RUNAWAYS

A True Story of Love and Danger

Jack and Zena Briggs

Introduction by John McCarthy

VISTA

A Vista Paperback
First published in Great Britain by Victor Gollancz in 1997
under the title *Jack & Zena*
This paperback edition published in 1999 by Vista
an imprint of Orion Books Ltd,
Orion House, 5 Upper St Martin's Lane, London WC2H 9EA

Typeset in Great Britain by Rowland Phototypesetting Ltd,
Bury St Edmunds, Suffolk
Printed and bound in Great Britain by
Clays Ltd, St Ives, plc

Acknowledgements

ZENA:
There are many people I'd like to thank: from those who were kind to us on our journey through to all those who have made this book come together.

In particular Debbie Jones, without whom only God knows where we might have ended up; profound thanks to Terry Waite who made so much possible; Mark Lucas, our agent, for his guidance and expert advice.

And from my heart I'd like to thank two special people: a man who's not only become a very special friend but whom I have come to love as a member of family – for having time, patience and just for being there, thanks John; and to the late Liz Knights, who made all this possible.

Above all, to my loving husband, for bringing me through all this – my love and life is for ever yours.

JACK:
To start with I'd like to thank my family, for never criticizing (especially my sister Jenny who had to live under extreme stress); John and Terry who listened, and most importantly understood, when many were on the fence and in the shadows – I feel privileged to call them friends. Mark Lucas for his expertise. Our friendly ghost who I am sure after therapy will be fine – thanks for your patience. The A-team at Gollancz for their support, in particular Liz Knights, without whom this book would not have been possible. My mother whom I shall love and miss for ever and a day. And to my wife, a very special woman, who has had to put up with so much, but has never stopped believing.

This book is dedicated to Mary

Introduction

When I met Jack and Zena I was surprised at how well they seemed – physically they both looked frail, but emotionally and intellectually they appeared very strong. As they told me their extraordinary story I came to know just how tough they have had to be. They spoke with great passion and with great humour – it was a moving and uplifting experience. Yet it wasn't until we parted that the horror of their situation became real for me.

Our meeting was a very rare outing for them; normally they sit at home, scared to go out, afraid every second they are in. While I was with them I remembered a recurring dream from my time in Lebanon. I would be out enjoying myself with family or friends until at some point I would always have to say, 'Well, I'd best be getting back now.' On waking I'd realize with distress that I was still a prisoner but would also be reassured that home was still my escape. In captivity home meant safety for me; to be there meant my ordeal would be over. For Jack and Zena, the nightmare continues wherever they are.

It is very hard to believe that this is happening in Britain today. But it is, and the story raises important questions about how we move on as a multiracial society. How can a family be free to plan to kill a daughter and the man she loves while the establishment appears unable or unwilling to work for a resolution? It is too simple to say that her family must just be made to drop their threats. Their actions come out of a cultural tradition that needs to be understood before it can be reformed. Reformed it must be for the sake of many other youngsters who wish to take up the personal opportunities of living in a multicultural society. It is vital for us to learn from this story to be better equipped to fight against racism. It is a tragic irony that it is Jack and Zena, the victims of this awful culture clash, who are the shining light of race relations in this situation.

Our society has not given them the support they deserve. This does not appear to be out of malice from the people in authority and, although there has been much incompetence in the handling of their case, it is the failure of society as a whole that represents such an important and disquieting aspect of this story.

One reacts, quite rightly, with anger to Jack and Zena's plight. But raging against the inadequacies of the system and condemning Zena's family with dismissive bigotry will gain us nothing. Again there is an irony in that the best example of some way forward is to be found with Jack and Zena. While angry, they have not become overwhelmed with bitterness. Zena remains a devout Muslim, with a commitment to her family and community. Jack remains proud of his wife's different background and traditions and is keen to understand them, as she is to understand his.

I do hope this book will provoke creative debate of the issues it raises. I believe it will. Above all, though, it is a testament to two remarkable young people. They sting the conscience while lifting the heart. They are still running scared, yet their courage can help us all.

JOHN McCARTHY
London, 1997

Preface: The Escape

My sister had told us we had ten minutes to say our final goodbyes. Then she'd banged the door behind her and I was alone with Jack.

I couldn't stop crying, I was hurting so much inside. Jack gave me a long hug – I didn't want to let him go. I looked into his face and told him I would always love him. Then I closed my eyes and asked him to kiss me. I didn't want to open them again till after he'd gone. I couldn't bear the thought of never seeing him again.

When he'd left, Miriam threw a complete wobbly. 'He's got you wrapped round his little finger!' she shouted. 'Don't you realize he'll leave you when he's got what he wants?' 'He's only after you for your money.' Horrible, hurtful things like that which I really didn't need to hear. Then she was threatening to tell my father and brothers exactly what had been going on all summer and autumn. 'If this isn't the end of it,' she said, 'if you haven't broken it off with him properly now, once and for all, I'll tell them.'

I ran upstairs to my little bedroom on the top floor. I climbed on to the bed just as I was and cried and cried. I loved Jack so much; he loved me, wanted to marry me. And yet we had to part, because I had been promised at birth to Bilal, who lived on a mountain in Kashmir. I had met Bilal only once when I was thirteen. It was so cruel and stupid and unfair.

Then I was lying face up, dry-eyed, watching the headlight beams of passing cars sliding across the ceiling. And suddenly I was thinking, I've got to go *tonight*. If I don't go now it'll never happen.

My bags were still packed from the failed attempt of earlier – I was all ready. I decided that I was going to make a break for it first thing in the morning, when my father and brother were back from the restaurant and asleep.

So I was off the bed and on to the floor getting ready. Making as little noise as possible I tore up the pile of sheets from my dressing-table drawer into long strips, then tied them together so I had four makeshift ropes. There was no way I was going to get down two flights of stairs carrying four bulky bags and not wake one of the family, so I'd hit on this plan of lowering them out of the bedroom window straight on to the pavement below.

Around four in the morning I heard my father and my younger brother Amir coming home. (My big brother Kasim slept with his wife in our other house down the street.) I listened as they washed and got ready for bed, and gave them an hour or so to be properly asleep. Then I slipped quietly into the Western gear I'd put ready on my bed: a pair of Amir's old jeans, which I'd got from the dustbin-bag on the landing where we used to leave clothes for the charity shop, and one of his striped shirts I'd taken from the ironing pile. Over this I pulled on a favourite Aran sweater of mine.

Then – it felt as if my heart was beating audibly – I pushed open my little window and shoved the first bag through. Though my father's bedroom was directly below mine, his window opened on to our side street, not the main road as mine did. So there was no way he was going to see the bags. But I was dreadfully scared that one of them would brush against the bricks of the wall and disturb him.

I had got to the end of my sheet-rope. I'd made it too short! The bag was swinging two feet above the pavement and I had to let it drop with a thump that sounded as if it would wake the dead. I waited a long minute to see if anyone was stirring – but no, it was all OK. Quickly but

4

carefully I lowered the other three bags on top of the first and tugged the window shut.

Well, this is it, I thought, taking a last hurried look round my bedroom. There by the bed were the family photographs: Dad, tall and distinguished as ever; my mother, her long hair now flecked with grey; Kasim, flashily dressed in one of his designer shirts; Miriam in happier days, smiling broadly; Amir, acting the typical lad as usual; finally my little sister Rani, grinning as she hugged my niece Mina.

There in the binliner was all my traditional wear, my *dupatta* and *shalwar-kameez*, still waiting for lazy me to iron them – now to be left behind for ever. There was my jewellery, in its box on the dressing table. I'd brought a little, but most I would have to leave. There on the stack system were all my old teenage albums – Madonna, Queen, Michael Jackson. The fun we'd had over the years dancing around the house to those! Dad had never minded us listening to Western music, as well as the Asian favourites we used to love.

But I'd made my decision – it was time to go. I was in such a state of nerves that I grabbed the wrong pair of boots, this old tatty pair I had in the corner, not the new ones I'd put ready. I knew I had to get out quickly now because my bags were sitting there waiting on the pavement.

As I tiptoed down the stairs in my bare feet my whole body was shaking. On the second floor I had to go right past both Dad's and Amir's doors. I knew every creak in the house, but if either of them woke, that would be the end of it. I'd be shipped back to Pakistan and Jack would have known nothing about it till my brothers came hammering on his front door.

Miriam was sleeping downstairs that night, on the couch by the TV in the dining room. (Dad had forgotten to take the front-door key down to the restaurant, so she'd had to stay there to let them in when they came home.) The

5

dining room was next to the front door so I couldn't risk going out that way. I'd decided I would have to climb out through the kitchen window.

I managed it, holding my breath as I swung my legs over the sill. But when I'd got out and was standing barefoot on the freezing pavement, I could *not* get the window closed again. The top aluminium rim kept getting caught on the lace curtain inside. Even though my arm was trembling so much I could barely hold it and I was desperate to get away, it had to be shut. It opened right on to the street at waist level. Some passer-by might have got in and woken my family. Then there was this old lady over the road who always got up early and would have been sure to ring the bell and say something.

It seemed like for ever, but eventually I got it shut enough, ran round the corner and found my stuff – the big black sports bag, the fluorescent rucksack and the two others. What did I think I was doing? As Jack said later, I'd brought everything but the kitchen sink.

When I'd got my boots on, crossed the main road and walked to the corner, I put this heavy luggage down for a moment. I turned and took one last look back at our house. I got this very strong feeling that that was it, the last I would ever see of my family. Leaving them was the hardest decision of my life. I knew full well what I was giving up. But I had to go. I loved Jack too much now to lose him.

I struggled down the road to this yard by the local furniture warehouse and unravelled all the long strips of torn sheet that were still tied to my bags. There was a big sign there on the wall saying NO DUMPING – £200 FINE. And here I am, I thought, leaving all these scrappy bits of cloth. Still, I hadn't got time to worry about that.

Round the corner was the local cab company. Luckily enough there was a car ready waiting. It was one of the young lads who'd sneaked me down to see Jack a couple of times before. As he put the bags in the boot he said, 'You're running for it, aren't you?'

I nodded. 'Yeah,' I said. He just grinned and when we had driven off he radioed back to base with a false name for me, and a false address for where I was going. He knew that Kasim was a close friend of the manager of the cab company.

'Good luck,' he said as he dropped me on the corner below Jack's mum's house – I didn't want him to know exactly which address I was going to. It was just starting to get light. I dragged the bags up the steep hill and knocked on the window.

1

ZENA:
My mother and father were both born in the Kashmir region of Pakistan, up in the mountains near the border with India. Dad came to England about forty years ago, to find work. Although we were from a high caste – the *jat-chadhuri* – there was only subsistence farming back home and he wanted something more.

So Dad bid his farewells to my mother and the rest of his family and friends and set off from our village. In those days the airport was a long trek away, and before he even got there news reached him that his father had been bitten by a rattlesnake. (He and his brothers had already lost their mother, and my grandfather had never remarried because he used to say that nobody could look after his three sons as she had done.) Hearing this, Dad hurried back, but there was no one who could remove the rattlesnake poison from my grandfather's body and he deteriorated very quickly. By the time Dad reached home he was dead.

My eldest sister Lamisha was only two at the time, a healthy, bubbly little girl. My grandfather was very fond of her and when he was dying he said he wanted her to be close to him. 'Don't hold her,' everybody in the village told him, 'because you'll pass the poison from yourself to her.' He told them not to worry, it would be OK; he wanted her near him because she was a part of his middle son who had gone away to England. Just before he died he said a strange thing. It didn't matter his holding his granddaughter, he told the village, because in forty days' time she would follow him.

And it came true: forty days after he died, Lamisha died too. It was a terrible shock for my father, losing both his father and daughter in such a short space of time. So when he finally arrived in England he was determined to make a success of his new start.

He worked initially as a foreman for the Yorkshire Foundries. When he'd settled in and found a home he applied for my mother to get a passport. Her application was successful, so she was soon able to join him.

My mother, though she was from the same caste as Dad, came from a much wealthier family. Her father had come over to England years before and had worked his way up to the point where he'd owned a fish and chip shop. He'd separated from my real grandmother and married an English lady. Her name was Beatrice – but more than that we never knew.

Soon after she arrived, Mum fell pregnant with my brother Kasim. After he was born Dad asked God for another daughter. Four years later his prayers were answered and Miriam arrived. Dad was so delighted that he held a foodgiving, where a lamb is sacrificed and given out to neighbours and friends in celebration. In our tradition this is a ceremony that is normally only held for a son. But Dad was so happy to have another daughter that he made an exception for Miriam. He gave up smoking and going to picture houses at this time. Obviously, this was partly to save more money for his young family, but it was also as a thank you to God for granting him another daughter.

These were all stories we used to be told when we were little, by both my mother and my father. And wrapped on the top shelf of the wardrobe in their bedroom by the three Holy Qurans was the shirt my grandfather had died in. It was cotton, with a Nehru collar, aged from white to a parchment yellow. There were still bloodstains on it, now very faded of course. I only saw it once, when we moved house; it was forbidden for us to touch it and it was never washed. For my father it held the smell of his father, and it brought him closer to his departed spirit.

Around the time I was born Dad was made redundant from the foundries and went to work for British Leyland. Eventually that job came to an end, too, when our local branch of the firm closed down. For a while he was unemployed and then he set himself up as a halal butcher. My father worked very hard all his life, supporting not just my mother and us but also his two brothers back in Pakistan, who had stayed farming the family smallholding and struggled to make ends meet. He sent money home to them regularly.

He is a handsome man, six foot two inches tall and very well built. His dark brown eyes are full of wisdom, though if you knew him as we did you would see in them the hardship he'd endured over the years. When we were young he was clean-shaven; later, after he'd returned from his pilgrimage to Mecca, he wore a beard, which was always nicely trimmed. He could be strict at times, but he never ever raised his hand to us. We just grew up knowing what was right and wrong. We respected his high standards and principles, so we never crossed that borderline where he might have had to discipline us.

This is not to say he lacked a sense of humour. He was always joking and laughing with us. He enjoyed many of the comedy programmes on the TV – his favourite being *Steptoe and Son*.

To us girls he was the perfect father figure. We always had the feeling that he was there to protect us, that we were safe and secure while he was around. When we were ill he brought us home grapes, or Lucozade and Ribena drinks. Even if it was just a headache, he'd make a fuss of you. 'Oh *no*,' he'd say in that lighthearted way of his, 'my daughter's *ill* today. I've brought her some of her favourite seedless black grapes.' Then he'd sit beside you and softly stroke the top of your head.

Once when I was about seven I had to go into hospital to have my appendix out. Dad came down to the ward

11

every night after work and sat by my bedside because I couldn't sleep if I was left on my own.

He was so generous in every other way, too. When we were kids, he opened an account at the sweetshop on the corner. If we wanted anything we could just run up the road and put it on tab. There were no other children we knew who were allowed to do that! When we grew older he'd bring back treats quite frequently: kilo boxes of pistachio nuts or almonds; then, when he started his butcher work, the finest quality meat – you'd never find an ounce of fat on the mince he brought home.

In return we daughters cooked for him and looked after him, though he was never the kind of selfish man who would expect you to tidy up after every last little thing he did. But it was our pleasure to care for him. We used to get up each morning to make sure he had his breakfast before he went out (he used to love my sunny-side-up eggs on toast). And if he came home and wanted food, even at two, three in the morning, we'd be happy to get up and prepare it for him. On his birthday we bought him aftershave; his favourites were Brut and Denim.

Sometimes Miriam and I would worry terribly about what would happen if he were ever to leave us. He'd always suffered terribly from ulcers, which could rile up at any time. Once Miriam found him collapsed at the bottom of the cellar steps. The only person in the neighbourhood that had a phone back then was the Asian clothes shop owner up the road. Miriam legged it up there and the ambulance came round and took him away. We were dreadfully scared then, not knowing what might happen.

But in hospital, as we sat around his bed, he reassured us. 'I'm going to be all right,' he said. 'I'm not going anywhere until you lot are grown-up.'

You'd never describe Dad as a soft touch, but it was my mother who mainly kept us in order at home. She was a very large woman physically, with a powerful presence to match, and although we knew she loved us, we also knew that there were certain things we couldn't get away with. She was stricter than my dad, more old-fashioned and traditional. She'd always make sure, for example, that we wore our *dupatta* headscarves when we went out. She would be insistent that we didn't talk to strangers. We certainly weren't allowed to sit out in the street chatting like all our neighbours did.

When my sister and I were in middle school we were put in long trousers rather than the short skirts the Western girls wore as uniform. But my mother insisted that that wasn't good enough, we had to wear the traditional *shalwar-kameez*, the baggy trousers and long loose top. She even made them up for us in the school colours of navy-blue and white.

She often told me that I watched too much telly. 'You need to grow up, Zena,' she'd say, and add that I should learn to pull my weight around the house. Then: 'You're spoiling her!' she'd tell my dad when he gave me money to buy things: clothes, or shoes, or magazines – *Smash Hits* and *Woman's Own* and *Cosmopolitan* and all the other stuff I used to love to read.

Shortly after my younger brother Amir was born Mum fell seriously ill with TB and had to go into hospital for some time. Kasim and Miriam were old enough to be at school in the day but I was too little and had to go into work with Dad (not that I have any memories of this – I was too young!).

Mum took a long, long time getting better. So from this time on, Miriam started to take on a large part of the role of mother around the house. She was only seven or eight, but already she was the one who looked after Amir and me. When we got up for school she would make our breakfast; in the evening she'd prepare the meal for the family and get us to bed. She ran the household and we younger ones looked up to her.

Obviously this was the result of particular circumstances, but it's traditional anyway, in Asian communities, for sons and daughters to help their parents as they grow up, take the stress off them and let them sit back a little.

That Miriam was often in charge didn't stop us two sisters being friends, though. We used to talk about everything. Last thing at night, when we'd made sure all the chores were done, we'd crash out in front of the TV, switch out the lights, put a movie on the video and tuck into pizzas and popcorn, chocolate and soft drinks.

At the weekend we used to have sixteen pints of milk delivered; Dad knew how much we enjoyed having a hot drink last thing before bedtime. Our Asian friends Henna and Elisa would come from down the street and we'd make almond milk or milk tea with cardamom and cinnamon.

As a family we were always close. Every night we sat round the table together for supper. Miriam would make a fresh curry, lamb or chicken or beef, with Adams butter, but always mild because of Dad's ulcers. Peppers and ghee were two things he had to avoid. Sometimes after we'd eaten Dad would go on down to the restaurant we had in town, other times he'd stay behind with us. Everyone was welcome, family or friends; he would never turn anyone away. On a cold winter's night the house would be full of the scent of cooking spices.

At home we spoke Urdu. We learnt Arabic, too, so that we could read the Holy Quran. And once I was thirteen I would observe the month of Ramadan with the rest of my family, staying inside, fasting and praying.

We never swore or talked about sex in front of our parents. If we were watching television with our father or mother and a sex scene came on we'd just quietly get up and leave the room. We never sat and watched together if that sort of thing was on.

Even though we wore our traditional dress to school and looked so different, there was very little racism. I can only remember one example and that was on my very

14

first day in middle school when we were fooling around in the playground and this girl shouted, 'Oh, look at that Paki!'

I went over to her. 'What did you say that for?' I said.

'D'you want a fight, then?' she replied, and pushed me. So I pushed her against the wall. She hit the back of her head, and the next thing I knew she'd collapsed on the ground. I wasn't to know that she got fits if she was knocked on the head! Anyway, my immediate reaction was to dive down and see why she wasn't getting up. A teacher came over and she was taken away.

The next day she was fully recovered. I went over to her and said I was sorry. I really didn't think I'd pushed her that hard. She apologized, too, for saying what she'd said. We shook hands and from that moment on became close friends.

When I first arrived at high school there wasn't a large percentage of Asians there. But by the time I was in my last year the quota had gone up enormously, as more and more Asian families moved into the neighbourhood. So whereas before I'd been alone among all the white English kids, the new Asian girls used to huddle together in a group. I noticed then that people would make snide or racist remarks about them, because they stayed in their group.

I was never hassled like that. My friends came from all over. I even had a Sikh friend, a young lass called Sophia who I used to bring home sometimes. Dad was quite happy with that, even though, of course, Sikhs and Muslims traditionally keep well apart.

As we grew older my English girlfriends started to have boyfriends. We never did. We had boys who were friends, obviously, but nothing more. You just knew you weren't allowed to, that it would cause terrible trouble if you did. Dad would be quite happy to let us walk home across the park with boys from school, but they were never allowed back to the house. Even if we had male relatives over they'd sit in one room and we'd be in the other. We'd only see them when we knocked on the door to bring them their tea.

After I left school at sixteen there was still no thought of a boyfriend. For a start we didn't go out to the places, like pubs and clubs, where we might have met one. Our brothers did; but for us girls it just didn't happen.

Obviously there was a part of you that thought, 'I wish I were there this evening . . .' Especially when your friends talked about the nights out they'd had. But you knew that even if you were invited out you stayed in. Sometimes we used to sit up with Henna and Elisa, watching videos till three in the morning, but it was always within the confines of the house.

In the third year of middle school – I must have been twelve, thirteen – we were told we were going back home to Pakistan for a holiday. Mum was going to take us two girls while Dad stayed behind with Kasim and his new wife, Nussarat.

We were very excited. About flying on a plane for a start. Then there were all these relations we'd heard about but had never seen. The one thing Miriam and I most wanted to do was visit our elder sister Lamisha's grave, as well as those of our grandfather and grandmother.

When we got there it was a huge shock. It was just so different. It was beautiful, certainly – the mountain scenery was magnificent – but there was such a vast amount of emptiness after what we'd been used to at home. You couldn't walk round the corner and find a chip shop!

We arrived first in my mother's village, which had small Western-style bungalows with standing taps outside. There was no running water or plumbed toilets, just a little cubicle where you washed with water you carried in.

After a day or two we went on up to my dad's village. It was a half-hour walk to a little bridge, then a narrow footpath up a hill so steep no car could drive there. The people lived in clay huts, and the cooking was done outside

16

on open stoves. There were no taps, they had to walk to the well to fetch water in buckets. There was no electricity, no telephones. To us, who'd grown up with deep-pile carpets and gas you could flick on and off with a switch, it was unbelievably primitive.

On our first night up there Mum introduced us to Salim and Bilal, the two sons of my father's elder brother. (It was their sister Nussarat who had married my older brother Kasim and now lived with us over in England.) Salim was in his late teens, a couple of years older than Miriam. To me, he seemed pretty arrogant. He had an amazingly old-fashioned attitude about women: if there was any housework or washing to be done, they should do it. Bilal, though only about sixteen, was the same. They even used to boss around their aunt, my father's younger brother's wife. She wasn't much older than them, and they used to tell her to wash their clothes or whatever. Mum told them not to, out of respect, and obviously when she was around they changed. But as soon as her back was turned, they'd return to their old habits. That was the way they seemed to carry on over there; they treated their women like slaves.

One day I was sitting outside one of the little huts in the morning sunshine, drawing a picture of our house back in England in the dirt with a bamboo stick. I put my father in too, standing to one side. We'd only been in Pakistan a few days but already I felt dreadfully homesick. Bilal strode over and scrubbed it all out with his feet. I couldn't believe what he'd done. I whacked him with the bamboo till he yelled.

One evening Mum took Miriam aside. 'We're going to have to get photographs of Salim,' she said, 'so we can apply for his visa.'

'Is he coming to stay with us?' Miriam asked.

'This is the man who's going to be your husband,' my mother told her. It was the first Miriam had heard of it and she was terribly shocked. But that is always the way

17

in our tradition. The subject of who you're intended for is never discussed, not even with your mother or father. To Westerners that may sound odd, but that's the way it is.

A couple of nights after that my mother said, 'We're going to need photographs of the younger one too.' Meaning Bilal. I didn't take in what she meant at the time. Later Miriam said to me, 'You know what that means, don't you?'

'No.'

'That one's for you. That's the one you're going to be marrying.'

'What d'you mean?' I replied. 'I'm too young.'

She shrugged. 'Well, that's why they want the photographs. That's the one you're going to be for.'

I couldn't believe it. He could barely speak English.

A few days after that the family took me back down to my mother's village because I was complaining so much. I couldn't cope with the life up there. No tap water, no electric light, and those rude lads. At least where my mother lived they had some amenities. And my mother's brother was OK. He was older and you could talk to him without feeling insulted.

Back in England Miriam applied for Salim's visa, and the preparations for her arranged marriage moved forward, slowly but inevitably. I knew all too well that once she'd been married off I was the next in line. Not for years, but I couldn't even bear the *thought* of Bilal.

Even then, as a young thirteen-year-old, I would lie on my bed in my little garret room and think, How am I going to get out of it? By my mid-teens I'd come up with this mad idea that if it ever came to it I'd pack a little bag with Western wear and run to our city centre. Down by the river I'd change out of my *shalwar-kameez* and *dupatta* and chuck them in the water. Then I'd make a dash for it, wearing the Western clothes, and when they found my traditional gear they'd think I'd jumped off the bridge and

18

killed myself. So they wouldn't come looking for me, wherever it was I ran to.

Then I'd think, What am I on about? At such a young age? It's against our religion to commit suicide and I didn't even want to think of dying; but set against that was my dread of marrying this man I despised. From the other side of the world. Who spoke barely any English. I couldn't stand the idea of going to bed with him, and in our culture rape doesn't exist within marriage. Once you're married you're there to make babies and that's it. (If they'd sent me back to Pakistan and forced me to marry him there's no way I could have gone to bed with that man – I would have had to push him down a well on the first day!)

I left school at sixteen without taking my exams. My father was very annoyed that I didn't finish my education and now of course I wish I'd listened to him, because those qualifications would be a massive help. But at the time they just seemed like pointless bits of paper. And I was upset with my parents because I'd been offered a place to go training with the under-sixteen England netball team and they wouldn't hear of it. Mum was worried about what our Asian neighbours would say about one of her daughters doing that. I'd regularly be in public out of traditional gear, wearing those very short netball shorts; and then also I'd be out late, mixing with other athletes in the evening, and so on.

I was terribly disappointed. It really brought home the strictness of the Muslim way of life. I lost heart about everything else then. If they wouldn't let me take this fantastic chance with my netball (which I loved) why, I thought, should I bother with the rest of it?

Then Salim had arrived from Pakistan. Miriam had fought his visa case for him, and later that year they were married in grand style. They had a seven-seater Mercedes limousine to take them from our house to the hall where the party was held. There were over four hundred guests present, from all over the UK.

Traditional wedding celebrations last for seven days. The bride's and groom's relations and all the Asians in the local community come round to the house. The women visit the bride on one side of the house and sing and throw money and put henna on her hands, and the men go to the groom on the other side, where they perform their customs.

On the wedding day itself the priest comes round and asks the boy, on his own, if he wishes to take the girl. The girl's father is present with the boy, who of course says yes. They then read a holy prayer. The same thing happens in another room with the girl. Then the wedding party drives in a procession to the hall.

The day was sadly marred for us by the sudden nervous collapse of my aunt. She'd been in and out of depression since her youngest child had been born, and we knew that crowds and noise upset her, but on the way to the party, in the bridal car, she suddenly turned to Miriam and said, 'If that bastard ever hits you we'll kill him.' It was clear she'd clicked into one of her states, so Mum took her back to the house. And I didn't get to the party till the end, because I had to stay behind at home with my aunt and her daughters. The next day she was admitted to hospital and seven days later she died. It was a terrible shock for us all, my mother, obviously, most of all.

After burying her sister Mum decided she had to return to Pakistan to look after her ageing mother. So Miriam was left to start married life with the extra burden of looking after us younger ones full time as well.

Her reaction to Salim had been very different from mine to Bilal. Over in Pakistan he'd been polite enough to her and they'd got on OK. They'd kept up a correspondence and all had seemed fine. And when he'd first turned up in England and my mother was around he'd behaved himself, obviously. But once he'd got married and Mum had gone back to Pakistan, it was as if he was a different man. He was difficult and arrogant, and he seemed to expect her to

20

cook and clean for him however she felt. (It wasn't only in our family that you noticed the transformation of these men who came over; among the women in our community it was often privately remarked upon. Was it because they felt insecure over here, we wondered, that they had to assert themselves in this way?)

The problem was made worse because Nussarat, Kasim's wife, was Salim's older sister. She was a lot older than Kasim: he'd been married to her when he was sixteen and she was in her late twenties. They had always rubbed along OK, and it was certainly true that Kasim loved his children. But nobody could ever say they were madly in love. Now, with my mum away, Nussarat used to gang up with Salim against us. If she was cross with Kasim she'd tell Salim and he'd take it out on Miriam.

It would happen like this: Kasim would stay out late one night and Nussarat would be angry. She'd have a go at him and he'd shout back at her, as usual, 'Oh, stop doing my head in, Nussarat, just leave me alone.' So then she'd go to Salim and tell him a load of crap she'd made up: that Kasim was swearing at her or hitting her, both of which things he never did. Or else she'd make up something about Miriam, that she'd seen her talking to this white man on the street, who she must be secretly in love with, already messing about with, and so on. Of course Miriam had white friends and might speak to them in the street, but that was it. When she came home Salim would grab her and quiz her: 'So who was he, then?' he'd say; or 'What is *he* to you?' (Nussarat resented Miriam anyway. I think she always thought that being older she should have been the woman of the house.)

Obviously it all came down to the clash of cultures, but living with this situation was a total nightmare at times. Where Salim came from, women knew their place and the men could do as they liked with them. He thought he had a God-given right to order us around, but we weren't going to stand for that. Neither me nor my brothers. 'Don't you

21

lay a finger on her,' we'd tell Salim if he got aggressive with Miriam, 'or we'll sort you out.'

There was even one time when Miriam was pregnant and Salim tried to push her down the stairs. Dad had bought a new house for us to move into, which we were all redecorating. If Amir and I hadn't been downstairs God knows what might have happened. We heard Miriam and Salim arguing upstairs. Amir ran up and when he got to the landing he saw that Salim had grabbed Miriam by the arm and was holding her above the top step. Amir got to him and pinned him against the wall. 'If you ever do that again,' Amir shouted, 'we'll sort you out so you'll never forget it!' But Salim just pushed him away with a sneery smile. He was just so cocky and arrogant. I rapidly grew to hate him.

He also refused to sit down and eat with us. At mealtimes he'd hide himself in his bedroom and come down and raid the fridge when it suited him. Dad used to tell him off but it never seemed to work. 'If you don't buck your ideas up,' he'd say, 'I'll send you back home to Pakistan.' But Salim just used to sit there nodding, and then he'd carry on as before.

About two or three months after Mum had been away in Pakistan my father started ringing her up asking for more photographs of Bilal to be sent over. I was now twenty years old and it was all too clear that the same groundwork was being laid for the event that I dreaded most in the world – marriage to Bilal.

Even though Dad knew Miriam's marriage was unhappy, there was no question of his changing his mind about this. To a Westerner, it might seem strange that I didn't try and talk it over with him, tell him that I *knew* that a union between myself and Bilal would be a disaster. But that's not the way we do things in our community. We'd never even raise our eyebrows to our parents, let alone question them. What they said went.

2

JACK:

When I think about the way I was before I met Zena it almost seems as if I was a different person. It's certainly true to say that falling in love with her turned my life upside down. Where would I be now, I sometimes wonder, if we hadn't met? Still ducking and diving on the wrong side of the law. Who knows, maybe even doing a five-year stretch?

I was born in a traditional back-to-back in a slum area of our northern city. We knew that's what it was because if TV companies wanted to film a slum area, ours is where they'd come. My dad was only married to my mother for a short while. He was a regular soldier and he left her, and us, when I was about seven. I barely remember him. When he'd gone she rarely talked about him. But it was clear enough from what she did say that their relationship had never been that happy.

She was a southerner, but when they split she took us kids up north, to where she had a brother. Her family hadn't exactly been wealthy, but they were comfortable enough. Her father was an international pharmaceuticals salesman in the 1920s and thirties. It was on one of his trips abroad that he met my grandmother, who was Belgian. There's a lovely old photograph of the pair of them standing in a European street – it must have been Brussels, I suppose – when they were young, he in his smart suit and tie, she all dolled up in the fashions of the twenties, with one of those spoon hats.

Her father was an officer in the war and rose to the rank

of major. When he came out he developed this poultice for burns – I don't know what it was exactly, but it had something to do with the mustard gas they'd used in the war. And by that stage he must have been more than a salesman because my grandmother always used to say that if only he'd held on to the patent we'd have been very rich.

What I do recall vividly, though, is the album full of stamps which my mother collected from the letters he'd sent her, with the weirdest designs from all over. Red Communist ones from Russia. Exotic wild animals and birds from Africa and the West Indies. Ma also had stories of how he'd turn up from abroad with coffee and tea and other luxuries that were rationed just after the war.

Gran followed my mother up north. By the time she died she had this lovely accent that was half Belgian, half Yorkshire. She taught us a lot – how to cook stews and soups, how to mend clothes, bits and bats of Flemish, all of which I've forgotten. I was a young teenage lad when she died. I have this memory of being sat in a pub with Ma and her brother just after we'd been to see her in hospital. 'What are we going to tell the children?' Ma said to my uncle.

'Is she dying?' I asked. 'Because if she is I want to know she is.' So they told me that she was – of cancer.

Besides Gran, my mother was the most important person in my life. She was deeply loved by all four of us children. She made a lot of sacrifices to feed and clothe us. She really fought tooth and nail for us when we were little. It can't have been easy for her, back then in the early 1960s, stuck alone in a back-to-back with four kids – especially with her southern accent.

She'd been a good-looking woman when she was young, with long auburn hair. She even did a bit of modelling at one time. But after my dad left there wasn't anyone in her life for a long time, apart from us. She wasn't the kind of mother who'd be forever introducing you to Uncle this and Uncle that.

We grew up fast. From a very early age I could cook, sew and clean. It was important to Ma that not only the girls but us boys did our fair share around the house. Looking back, it must have been hard on her because she had to take on two roles – on the one hand a father, a disciplinarian; on the other a comforting, supportive mother.

Broken families were less common in those days, but we weren't the only one in our area. I had this friend from school, Gavin, and whenever we went down to his house there'd just be his mother. 'My father's asleep,' he'd say. It wasn't until I was about seventeen that he actually got round to telling me the truth. That his father, too, had left when he was a young lad. We'd all realized the truth, though, and when I asked why he hadn't told me, he said his mother had been insistent that he mustn't let it out that his dad had gone.

I grew up much like any other northern working-class lad. When we weren't at school I'd be off with my mates playing football in the big local park. On summer days there'd be a whole gang of us. On a weekend we'd be out there from ten in the morning till eight at night. One of the great things for the kids in our area was boogie-building. 'Boogies' were carts made from a plank of wood with pram wheels. We used to race them down this long steep road, steering with two lengths of string. We were lunatics, piling on four or five to a boogie, dodging down the road through the passing cars. There were no brakes, just our feet, clad in these cheap plastic sandals we all wore, known as Pashley Specials. In summer these used to melt in the heat and stick to the tarmac.

My brother Ryan was three years older than me, and my sister Karen four. That was quite a gap when we were kids. They had their own set of friends, and I desperately wanted to tag along with them but they knew what I was like – if we went somewhere we weren't supposed to, or something went wrong, I'd straight away be back home to tell Ma. So one of Karen and Ryan's tricks was to take me aside and say, 'Oh, Jack, Mum's got some sweets for you at home.' So off I'd trot – gullible idiot – and they'd scarper with their mates.

As we grew up, though, Ryan and I became good friends, even if we did wind each other up the whole time. I remember coming home from school once and there was a massive removal van parked outside our house. I knew Ryan had recently got himself a job but I didn't know what it was.

'Do us a favour, our kid,' he said when I came into the kitchen.

'What?'

'Get us me cigs from the van.'

'Is that *your* van?' I said, amazed.

'Yeah, yeah,' Ryan nodded, proudly. 'Me cigs are on the dashboard. Just nip out and get 'em, would you?'

I went out and I was just climbing up over the seat to get them for him when the real van-driver turned up. He was a huge brawny fellow.

'Hey!' he shouted. 'Where the fuck d'you think you're going?'

'I'm just getting our kid's cigs.'

I turned round and Ryan was at the front window of our house, pissing himself. The van was nothing to do with him, of course.

My other sister, Jenny, was four years younger than me. As a child she always seemed to have her nose in a book. Historical novels were her favourite. I think we first started to become close when I was about eleven and we had to go and stay with our gran while the council put a bathroom and inside toilet in my mother's house. It was like a little adventure for us two – we slept on camp beds at one end of Gran's bedroom.

Eleven-plus came by and quite a few of the lads I knew passed and went off to the grammar school. I never saw them much after that. I failed and went to secondary modern, where I stayed until I left at sixteen, without a qualification to my name. They'd sent me off on day-release to building college, but I got thrown out for lighting a smoke bomb outside the headmaster's study. He didn't see the funny side of it at all, and when I think about it now I can see his point. He was trying to help us and I was just another annoying teenager – a real rebel without a clue.

As far as I was concerned the Real World lay outside the school gates and I couldn't wait to leave. I got a job almost immediately, as a warehouseman to a bullion dealer. But I soon realized that that wasn't what I wanted out of life and I left after a short while. I just didn't want to be the kind of person of whom you could say he was born, lived and died in the same spot, he got his gold watch after fifty years. I wanted something more.

I remember a mate of mine pointing at a back-to-back in the street just down from our home. 'I've just started on my mortgage,' he said, 'and in twenty-five years' time that place'll be mine.' Now that I'm older I realize what a fantastic commitment that is, but at the time I just laughed. 'I don't know whether I'm still going to be in this job in twenty-five *minutes*,' I replied, 'let alone twenty-five years.'

So I fell into a life of ducking and diving, earning a bit here and a bit there, signing on in between times. Soon enough I got involved in petty crime. It started when I was skint and this mate of mine, Keith, said, 'Well, we could get ourselves a few quid if you fancy it. We could go out and do a few telephone boxes.' He was already well experienced in how to go about it. It was easy enough. You just jemmied the cashbox off and helped yourself. (The phone would stay in working order but when you put a coin in it would fall to the floor. People wouldn't report them for ages because they used to get free phone calls.)

Some of the boxes had thirty or forty quid in them, which was a lot of money back then at the end of the seventies. The worst problem was the noise you made when you walked into a pub because all you had on you was ten-pence pieces. But we always made sure the phones were still working. If they weren't we'd phone and report it. It was always at the back of my mind that someone might need the phone in an emergency, and that if it was broken it could cause a lot of trouble.

We did about thirty of them and then, inevitably, we got caught. We were taken to court and I seriously thought I'd go to prison. I was extremely lucky and got community service, as did Keith.

After that I kept out of trouble for a while. In between stints on the dole I did any number of things: potato picking, gravedigging, labouring, whatever came along. For a while I worked in the flies of the big theatre in town. That was a great experience, the first time I'd felt really happy in a job. You met a lot of famous people and though the pay was terrible it was a good way of pulling the girls. They had some crazy romantic notion that working in the theatre meant you were glamorous.

When the panto season was over and I was thrown out of work, I fell back to less legit activities. I got allocated a council flat which I ended up sub-letting as a brothel. I used to get so much a day – ten, twenty quid. It was a pittance when you consider the amount of business they were doing in there, but it was enough to keep me ticking over. The way I looked at it was that I wasn't really using the flat so it seemed like a good idea that someone did. In no way was I ever the classic pimp with the broad-brimmed hat and the fingers dripping with gold, but my name was on the rent book and the law is, whoever's name is on the rent book is held responsible.

One day I called up the flat and they told me the place had been busted. I managed to avoid the Old Bill for a week but in the end I got fed up with it, went down and handed myself in. These two officers put me in an interview room and I tried to pretend I hadn't known what the place was being used for. One of these coppers was a real cocky bastard. 'Come *on*,' he was going, 'we found four hundred durex in the flat. You're not telling me they were all for personal use? And a cupboard full of leather dresses. We're either going to charge you with being a brothel-keeper or a raving bloody transvestite.'

They charged me with 'allowing premises to be used' and I lost the flat. The council, obviously, weren't too thrilled with my use of it. Once again I was lucky enough to escape imprisonment and I was fined two hundred pounds. How I was meant to pay this amount without a job I don't know.

One day I was at my mother's and there was a knock at the door. I opened it and outside stood this guy who looked like a mixture between Boris Karloff and the Hunchback of Notre-Dame.

'Are you Jack Briggs?'

'Yeah.'

'Right, you're under arrest.'

'What d'you mean I'm under arrest?'

'I'm a warrant officer, and I'm here to charge you for non-payment of a fine of two hundred pounds. Don't worry,' he went on as I stood there reeling, 'it's all right, because what I'm going to do is instantly bail you and tell you that you have to appear in court.' On such and such a date, he said. So I appeared in court again. Again I promised I'd pay off this fine at so much a week.

But unfortunately I never managed to find the money. So ensued this chase. This Boris Karloff warrant officer must have been part Canadian Mountie because he always seemed to be out and about looking for me. Sometimes it felt as if I was the only person in the whole city who owed a fine. He called at my mother's again, only this time I'd peeked through an upstairs window and I knew it was him. My mother opened the door and said, 'I'm sorry, he's not here.' Fifteen minutes later I thought it would be safe to go out. The crafty git had only gone and parked at the top of our street. Now he came zooming down the hill after me. Seeing him, I jumped over the wall into the neigh-bouring school yard and belted off. His car screeched to a halt and he shouted after me, 'Stop! I'm an officer of the law!' I couldn't stop laughing. It was like something out of an Inspector Clouseau film. I was laughing so much that I nearly didn't get away.

Eventually they must have decided this warrant officer was never going to catch me, so they sent the Old Bill after me. I was sitting in one of my locals one evening and the doors flew open and in marched four officers with handcuffs. There was no escape from them. I was arrested and taken to the main city jail.

It was my first-ever taste of being banged up. After I'd been charged I was taken downstairs and left on a bench in this long cage full of prisoners. It was like a corridor with bars, and there were all sorts in there. I'd managed to get a phone call through to my brother Ryan to tell him what had happened. 'What I'm going to do,' he told me, 'is I'm going to try and raise the money to bail you. If I can't, I'll drop you off some tobacco. So you'll know either way.'

So I was sitting there surrounded by all these desperate characters and this screw came strolling down shouting out my name. Oh, brilliant, I thought, our kid's raised the money. But he came up and pushed half an ounce of Golden Virginia through the bars, so I realized I was done for, the fine wasn't going to get paid for me, and I'd be sent up to the big jail, which is notorious in our county.

Right, I said to myself, you've got to prepare yourself mentally. I had visions of the film *Stir Crazy* where Gene Wilder and Richard Pryor are absolutely crapping themselves because they're about to be banged up. Richard Pryor says, 'Look, you've got to act tough because if you look tough they won't touch you.' So I was thinking I'd better put on this big bravado act, pretend that I was used to this kind of thing and that it wasn't bothering me.

While I was sitting there the door to the cage opened and in came this immaculate city-slicker type, complete with charcoal-grey suit, Crombie hat, briefcase and umbrella. I think we all thought at first that he was some-one's brief. The door clanged shut and everyone went deadly quiet. He was a prisoner all right. But here was someone who'd clearly never been in a police station in his life, let alone locked up in a cell. I shuffled down the bench next to him. This is going to be good, I thought.

'So what's your story?' I asked.

'You wouldn't bloody believe it, I was on my way to work this morning and I got stopped by the traffic police. My wife's apparently put out this order of maintenance so they've arrested me. Made me feel like a bloody criminal.'

Everybody just stared at him. About ninety per cent of the people in that crowd *were* bloody criminals.

I was expecting to be called up to court, but instead this screw came in, handcuffed me to this other lad and we were bundled into this Black Maria and taken to the main jail. Shit, I thought, this is it. I'm finally going up there.

The first thing that hit me was the noise. It was unbeliev-able. People screaming and swearing at each other, foot-steps clattering up iron staircases, the clanging of doors, screws yelling, all amplified by the four walls enclosing you. It was like a city within a city. It took about six hours to go through what they called Reception. There were forms to be filled in, and then a medical where you were stripped naked and made to wait in a queue until this doctor looked you over front and back, tapped you twice on the chest and pronounced you OK.

I was there for four days. Then all of a sudden my cell doors were flung open. 'Get your kit,' said this screw, 'you're going.' I thought I was about to be moved to another jail but in fact my brother had managed to raise enough to pay off the remainder of my fine, so I was free.

That experience left a very strong impression on me. I realized that if you were going to get involved in crime either you had to be extremely clever and not get caught, or you had to leave it alone. I decided to leave it alone. I wasn't cut out to be a criminal.

Which is not to say that everything I did from then on was completely legit. But I made sure I never did anything I could be sent to jail for.

I worked at what you might call the dodgy end of the clothing industry. Sometimes within the business there are sales for the people who work in a factory – of garments that might be classed as seconds, or in a fashion line that has become redundant. I got myself into a position where I could get my hands on such stuff and sell it on. What I was doing never did anyone an ounce of harm. If someone wanted to buy a Hugo Boss top which had a label in it saying Hugo *Bass* that was fine by me. Nobody was losing their job, nobody was getting undercut, these clothes would have been sold anyway. Meanwhile the punters were getting a nice cut-price top. Everybody was happy.

And so life went on, from deal to deal, from month to month, from year to year. And I'm quite sure that if I hadn't seen Zena, striding so confidently down the street that sunny summer's day, nothing much would have changed.

3

ZENA:

I can remember vividly the day I met Jack. It was a beautiful summer's morning, and I'd been sitting outside on the door-step of one of the houses in our street, chatting away with our regular group of friends: Henna and Elisa, a young English couple, Dean and Tracy, who lived up the street, and this thirtysomething bloke, Colin, who was also local.

We used to have the door open and music blaring out from inside the house. It must have been on a weekend because I remember that all the younger kids were playing around us, screaming up and down and having fun as usual.

We were having a discussion about what we would look for – in an ideal world – in a man or a woman. I was saying that what I'd like was a man with ripped jeans, a leather jacket and a 1000cc Harley-Davidson.

Suddenly I felt this tap on my shoulder and this bloke Colin was laughing and saying, 'Look, he's here, but without the Harley-Davidson!' I turned round and there was Jack. He was wearing ripped jeans and a leather jacket! We all started to laugh. I'd only seen him once before – he'd waved to me in the street, which I'd thought was odd as I didn't know him. Now, though, he seemed completely normal – relaxed and friendly, joining in our laughter. He introduced himself as the uncle of Adrian and Scott, who were two of the local kids, so we knew immediately who he was.

Most afternoons that summer we used to take all these children to a park which was a five-minute walk away, at the bottom of the main road that ran past the end of our street. We'd troop down there in a huge gaggle. Some days Miriam would come, other days Henna. Her parents were more liberal and Westernized than ours. Sometimes she and Elisa would be allowed to go out in the evening to a Bhangra do (where Indian music is played and all sorts of people, English and Asian, mix and socialize). So there was always plenty for us to gossip about. We'd sit and chat as we played with the kids – football for the older ones, roundabouts and slides for the babies.

Now Jack took to coming along too. He was great with the children, brilliant at larking about and making them laugh. In between times we'd quite often find ourselves talking. There was no romance about it at first, just a friendship – although I'd be lying if I denied that right from the moment when I turned round and saw him standing there I did fancy him a little. There was something rugged about his looks; his face just told you he'd seen life, lived it, and then he had those lovely blue eyes – the blue of the ocean, I always used to think.

Some afternoons I'd see him sitting on the steps outside his sister Jenny's house. So we used to continue our conversations there, though I'd always make sure I was off the street before Dad came home. If Mum had been around it would have been absolutely forbidden for us to go out and mix in the street. With Dad it was just generally agreed that when he walked round the corner from the bus stop we'd be back at home. I don't think he minded that much himself, but he certainly wouldn't have wanted other people within the Asian community making remarks about his daughters being out and about, talking to men from outside the family. It's all too easy for Asian girls to get branded as 'dirty property'; then they may be rejected by their fiancé's parents and bring shame on their family. A daughter, basically, has to make sure that there is never even the faintest reason for slander against her; she has to be totally pure.

It's hard to remember exactly how this friendship with Jack developed into a serious romance. Something just slowly clicked in me. It was partly his sense of humour, the way he made me laugh and feel good. I was also intrigued by his past; I loved listening to the stories he had to tell about the things – some of them pretty dodgy – that he'd got up to over the years. And he was obviously kind; to me, that just shone out of him. Gradually, as the summer went on, I realized I was starting to feel something more for him.

It was terribly hard, then, because I felt as if I would never be able to express my feelings to him. I thought that if I said, 'Jack, I think I'm falling in love with you,' he might not want to see me any more. Especially if he were to realize what my family would think, if it ever happened and they found out. I knew that for my family it was completely out of the question for me to marry anybody but Bilal. Girls who resisted the system – who ran away, even with other Asian men – were ruthlessly hunted down and brought back. They and their families would be in disgrace. Sometimes it didn't stop there. There were stories you heard, or even occasionally read in the press, where women were crippled or murdered for their disobedience. In our city, just recently, one young girl who'd been seeing someone she ought not to had been run over three times and killed by her brother-in-law. That had made the newspapers. And privately, within the community, you heard of many other examples. More often than not the disobedient woman would be taken back to Pakistan and nothing more would be heard of her.

There was also the more practical problem – that I couldn't do the things he, as a Westerner, would expect of me, as a girlfriend. I couldn't go out at night, to pubs or clubs, or do any of the things he was used to. So I told myself, over and over, not to fall in love with him. But I still went on seeing him. I couldn't help it. I suppose I'd managed to convince myself that we were just good friends.

We were so often in a group or with the kids. It wasn't a[s] if it was just us two, always alone together.

Then one day Jack wanted to go and see a movie – i[t] was *Basic Instinct*, I remember. Nobody else in the grou[p] was interested in going, so I said, 'Well, if nobody els[e] wants to go, Jack, I'll come with you.' We had to be s[o] careful, even on that one trip. If any of my relatives ha[d] seen us out together in town it would have got bac[k] immediately to my brothers and father and that woul[d] have caused havoc. We girls always had complete freedom within the house, but outside, certainly as far away as th[e] city centre, I was supposed to go either with Miriam o[r] one of my brothers.

I'd never been to a picture house before. All the film[s] we'd watched had been on the video at home. It was brilli-ant, seeing the action on the big screen – it was a much larger space than I'd ever imagined. As a child, I'd been brought up to think the cinema was a bad place. I couldn'[t] see what the fuss was about – with the sweet counter an[d] the popcorn machine it just seemed like good clean fun t[o] me. When we'd found our seats and sat down, Jack starte[d] on about how the film had, as he put it, 'a very adul[t] theme'. I think he thought that just because we wore tra-ditional dress we were backward! Afterwards we went fo[r] a coffee in town. It was the first time I'd ever been on [a] date and, though I was dreadfully worried I might be see[n] by somebody, I was enjoying every minute of it. We too[k] a taxi back because I didn't want to risk us being caugh[t] together on the bus. I walked five yards behind Jack unti[l] we found a taxi. Obviously we had to make sure the drive[r] was white. Then when we got back to our area I droppe[d] him off quite a distance from our street.

A couple of days later we were alone together in th[e] park, just mooching around on one of the benches by th[e] swings and roundabouts, watching the kids from a dis-tance. He suddenly stopped his usual banter and wen[t] quiet. 'Look, Zena,' he said eventually. 'I don't know ho[w] to put this, but I think I'm feeling a little bit more than just friendship here.'

So at last I was able to tell him that I'd been feeling the same, all along. 'I didn't want to say anything,' I said, and I explained why, exactly what it would mean if we were to start a relationship. 'We won't be able to walk down the street holding hands and kissing,' I told him. 'That can never happen. And if anybody finds out, the ultimate price we'll have to pay is our lives.'

Again I explained how seriously our Asian community took arranged marriages; about the shame it would bring and the danger we'd be in from my own family if we were ever discovered. My brothers might seem easygoing enough on the surface, but I knew all too well how they would react if family honour was called into question.

Just a few months before, on Valentine's Day, I'd received an anonymous card. Miriam, Henna, Elisa and I had laughed about it. We didn't know who it was from and I'd done nothing to encourage it, but we knew nonetheless we'd have to keep it a secret from my brothers. But somehow Kasim found out. He came home one evening and went crazy, swearing and screaming at me, demanding to know where the card was. We girls all tried to deny I'd received it. But he went on so much that I gave in eventually and showed it to him. He was trembling with rage as he held it. 'I'll sort him out,' he muttered. 'And then,' he turned to me, 'I'll find out why he sent it.'

'I don't know who it's from,' I protested. 'I really don't.'

'Oh, Kasim, it's just a joke,' Miriam chipped in.

'We'll see about that,' said Kasim, and turned on his heel.

I told Jack about this, and other, much more serious stories I knew. There'd been the case of a distant cousin of mine who'd fallen in love with a young Sikh girl. One day it leaked to her family that they were seeing each other. This cousin came running to our house with a suitcase full of the girl's clothes: her perfume and make-up and slippers.

He was terrified that if her brothers raided his house they'd find them. He couldn't even risk leaving them with close relatives of his, for fear the Sikhs might visit them, too. That young girl vanished from England. She was taken home and never heard of again; the rumour was they'd done her in. Meanwhile her family here vowed revenge on our cousin. 'We'll get you one day,' they warned, 'no matter how long it takes.'

One day this cousin was on his way back from work. He'd just got off the bus in our area when he saw them, six or seven of her brothers and cousins, all tooled up with the traditional knives they're allowed to carry. They chased him up this steep hill. He'd decided to run that way because he knew there was a big family of Muslims who lived at the top. They were notorious, these brothers; there were seven of them, and nobody messed with them.

Just before he got to their house these Sikhs caught up with him. He was screaming for the brothers as they set upon him. Luckily the brothers heard, came out and chased the Sikhs away, but by that stage they'd managed to hack my cousin's shoulder blade clean off and split the back of his head open with an axe. He was lucky to survive, and certainly he'd have been killed if those brothers hadn't been there to defend him.

This was just one of the stories I told Jack. When I went home that evening I thought, Right, that's it, I've gone and put him off the idea completely. But the next thing I knew was he'd called round to talk to Miriam and discussed it all, and asked if he could take me out. At that stage she didn't seem to mind. I think she thought it would just be a light-hearted summer romance, and when winter came and Mum returned from Pakistan it would fade away. Miriam knew that I knew where my destiny lay; in the end I would have to do what was expected of me. 'We've been through it,' she'd say to me whenever we got into a discussion about arranged marriages, 'so you can go through it too.'

But she was mistaken. Our trips with the kids to the local park were replaced by walks along the canal, and by meetings in a big park near the city centre (both of which were places less frequented by the Asian community). Sometimes we'd go round to Jack's mother's place, also in another part of town. Mary was a lovely warm person, who immediately accepted me as Jack's girlfriend.

By September it had got to the point where I was lying to Miriam, telling her that I was going to traditional sewing classes at a local community centre for Asian women when I was actually seeing Jack. As soon as I was out of the house I'd run down to the local cab line and get a taxi over to our meeting place. There was this one old driver, Derek, who would generally take me. After a while, he knew we were seeing each other, and he knew what would happen if anything leaked out, so he always used to say, 'Make sure you ask for me.'

Jack and I used to talk and talk and talk. About this, that and everything. TV programmes, music, food, current affairs, you name it. At first he had been quite awkward, as if now that we had moved from friendship to relationship we were testing each other out. But as we got to know each other better we became more and more relaxed.

Jack was fascinated about my background. He wanted me to tell him all about my culture and traditions: about Pakistan, about the way Asian families look after each other, about our Muslim religion, what it felt like having your marriage arranged for you by your parents.

By the time the leaves were turning brown and piling up on the pavements I knew for definite that he was the man I wanted to spend the rest of my life with. Having decided that, I had to start facing up to the fact that if he felt the same way about me I would have to make the ultimate choice – between Jack and my family. I knew only too well I couldn't have both.

JACK:

We met in the summer of '92. My younger sister Jenny had a house in the same street as Zena. It was a classic row of northern back-to-backs, three storeys high, in dirty red brick. On Jenny's side there were little front gardens and a flight of steps leading up to the front door. On Zena's side you just walked straight in off the street.

Jenny lived there with her husband Dan and their two little boys, Adrian and Scott. Jenny had grown up to be a home-loving person, and her house was always a nice place to stop by. My own flat was pretty well unfurnished at the time – just a crash pad with a dusty old settee and a cooker – so I used to be up at Jenny's quite frequently.

It was a really beautiful summer that year. Remembering it now, it reminds me of that film of Spike Lee's, *Do the Right Thing*. It was just that kind of feel. People were out in the street the whole time, sitting on their doorsteps with ghetto blasters, playing music, having a can of Coke or a can of beer. When the summer holidays came everyone used to keep an eye on everyone else's kids.

A few minutes' walk away down the main road there was a park. Sometimes, to help Jenny out, I used to take Adie and Scott down there. Quite often Zena'd be there with her nieces and nephews, so all of them used to play together in a big group. Then we got into the habit of going down together and picking up a whole lot of other kids on the way. It was a great time, heading to the park in the sunshine with this gaggle of screaming kids all around.

At the beginning, Zena and I just used to talk. Although we were from completely different worlds we soon found out that we could make each other laugh. We had a lot in common. It was really no more than a friendship to start with. Apart from anything else, I wouldn't have thought I'd have stood a cat in hell's chance with her in any other way. She was so beautiful, so bubbly, she had such a lovely, lively personality. I was ten years older, was starting to lose my hair, and I'm hardly an oil painting to start out with. Quite apart from which, she was from this completely different culture. I'm not prejudiced – my mates have always been from all over, and if there's one thing I despise it's a racist – but you knew that Asian women were something different. They came from this very tight, closed community and were married off within that community. So you just didn't think of them in that way.

I remember the first time I saw her. She was walking down the street on her own. She just looked so confident, as if she hadn't got a care in the world. It was her whole nature, the way she carried herself that was so attractive. It was almost as if she owned the street. She had no make-up. Just these flashing brown eyes and this incredible mass of thick black hair. I don't know whether it had anything to do with me losing mine, but it was very, very appealing. Just the sheer volume of it, and the way it tumbled right down her back to below her little waist. She was gorgeous-looking.

I know that Asians regard Western dress as provocative, but to me the traditional dress she wore was beautiful too. They call it *shalwar-kameez* – trousers and top. She had this one outfit in a caramel-coloured kind of georgette material. She looked just stunning in that.

As the summer wore on we met up more and more often. I found Zena so refreshing, so completely different from the sort of women I'd been used to in the past. She had no interest in pubs or nightclubs or anything like that. It was lovely to see a woman without make-up, who was so natural, and had such a zest for life. That captivated me straight away.

Maybe the fact that she wasn't from the world I knew made her more attractive. I remember when I first took her out, and we went to see *Basic Instinct*, I was really worried that she was going to be shocked. The cinema was almost empty, and as the opening credits rolled, and we sat there watching Sharon Stone rogering away with

41

Michael Douglas, I had a vision of this little bundle of *shalwar-kameez* just running screaming out of the main door. But she was a lot more knowing than I'd realized. Though she and her sister had always been confined to the house, they'd always had the freedom to watch whatever TV or videos they liked.

When I got my courage up, and very nervously and tentatively suggested one afternoon in the park that we might be more than just good friends, I was all set for a slap on the face. But my gut feeling had been right. She felt the same way about me.

Right at the start she was very forthright about what I was getting myself into. She explained that there was no way she'd be allowed to go out in the evening to pubs or clubs. If we were to have a relationship it would have to be completely secret. If her dad or her brothers discovered, it would be highly likely that she'd be on the first plane back to Pakistan and I'd get beaten up.

She told me a number of tales about what had happened to couples who had been found out. I didn't exactly think that she was embroidering the truth, but at that stage, though these stories did scare me, they didn't put me off. One, we weren't going to get found out. Two, I've always thrived on the edge. The vague threat of a beating wasn't going to stop me seeing this girl who was not only so beautiful and nice-natured, but with whom I got on better than any woman I'd ever met before.

I'm also the kind of bloke who doesn't respond well to being told that something isn't allowed. In part I suppose it's a natural rebelliousness – it's like a child being told 'Don't touch that'. The child is immediately going to want to touch whatever he's been forbidden. There was, if I'm honest, something of that in my response to what she had told me.

Which is not to say that I didn't think about the whole thing pretty long and hard. Before I'd even asked her out to the cinema I'd been up to see Miriam to get her permission to take Zena out. She'd given me the OK. Although she'd warned me about their brothers, and explained that even though I got on well enough with them as acquaintances, if they thought I was seeing their sister in any romantic way I'd be in serious shit.

Now I went to see Miriam again, to explain my feelings and to say that I wanted to start seeing Zena as a girlfriend. I was very surprised when Miriam said she thought that would be absolutely fine. Again came the warning about the brothers, but otherwise no objection at all. I think she thought that it was just going to be like a little summer romance, a bit of innocent fun for Zena.

But when autumn started to draw in, my feelings for Zena were growing stronger than ever. It's hard for someone like me to put this kind of thing into words. I'd had plenty of girlfriends in my thirty years, and been in love before, in a way. But what I was starting to feel for Zena eclipsed all that. She was everything I'd ever wanted, and more.

Before, I suppose, it would have been natural to get into a physical relationship pretty quickly. Now, I found myself easily accepting that for Zena sex was something that didn't happen till after you were married. She was just different, in every way.

We used to meet either at my flat or, more often, up at my mother's, then head out for long walks along the canal or to the main city park. My mother accepted Zena straight away, as did Ryan and my sisters. I said something like, 'I've met this woman and she's really nice and she's Asian.' They didn't bat an eyelid about her race or colour.

On our walks we'd chat away to each other non-stop. Sometimes we'd daydream about what it would be like to have a place of our own, or what it would be like if we could express our affection openly. We couldn't hold hands or kiss in the street, obviously. As soon as we were back in our area we had to be strictly apart. If she went up the street with her dad, and I was out in Jenny's front garden,

43

she'd have to ignore me. Unless of course her father said hello to me. But even then Zena and I never made eye contact.

ZENA:
I had this secret life with Jack going on and although I was increasingly anxious about how it would all turn out in the end I was deliriously happy inside.

It was quite a contrast to the rest of my family. That summer and autumn things had really deteriorated between Miriam and Salim – to the point where she'd actually thrown him out of the house. (We'd moved up the road by now, and left Kasim and Nussarat alone together in the old house, so Salim stayed with his sister for a while.)

He was impossible. He wasn't working, in the restaurant or anywhere else, but he'd stay out late, lazing around at relatives' houses, then in he'd waltz the next morning and say, 'Where are the clothes I wanted washing?' or, 'Cook my dinner.' He used to treat Miriam like some kind of slave. I couldn't bear it. As well as looking after us, she was bringing up their daughter, Mina.

But people in the neighbourhood started making up these terrible stories about her so she was forced to take him back. It was crazy; they were Asian families who were saying these things. They never looked into their own backyard to see what their own daughters were up to. It was easier for them to point the finger at us. It didn't help that Nussarat was very popular in the local community. She'd obviously tell the story with her own bias and these gossiping women would believe it.

When Jack used to take his two nephews to school he'd sometimes run into Miriam with Mina. Jack was good with kids and some of these women would see him with Mina and go back to Nussarat and say, 'Miriam treats that white man more like a father to Mina than she does her own husband.' It wasn't Miriam's fault if Salim was so selfish that he couldn't even be bothered to take his own daughter to school. And then Nussarat would stir it with Salim. 'Why's your daughter going to school with *him*?' she'd say. On one occasion Salim got so angry with Miriam he slapped her one, right in front of me while she was doing the washing-up. Miriam can be tolerant but she's got her breaking point. After Mina was born she'd suffered badly from depression, and she hadn't been her old self for some time. Now she spun round with what she'd been washing held tight in her hands: in one the pressure cooker, in the other a big knife.

'Come on,' she screamed and her eyes were crazy. 'Come and get me!'

He dropped his arm and backed off. 'I'll get you two one day,' he was saying, shaking his head from side to side. 'When you get married,' he added to me, 'we'll have both of you.'

It was something he repeated frequently; because he knew I was the cocky one of the two of us and one day I'd be wed to Bilal. When that day came, he reckoned, they'd have us where they wanted us.

'There's nothing your lot can do to me,' I used to reply.

'Yeah, there is,' he'd say. 'When you get back to Pakistan we'll sort you out good and proper.'

I used to stand my ground with him, but when he said those things it sent shivers down my spine. It's true, I used to think. If they send me back to Pakistan what will I do? If I'm married off to Bilal that's it – I'm done for. The photographs of Bilal had arrived by this stage. He was the double of Salim, which made me loathe the prospect even more.

One evening late in October we were sitting in the kitchen at home, all of us girls together: Miriam, me, Henna and Elisa. There was a knock at the front door and it was Jack.

'Oh, hello,' I heard him say as Miriam answered the door. 'Can I have a word with Zena?'

'Come on in, Jack,' she replied. She was still happy with him being around me at that time.

He wanted to talk to me in private, he said, so we went through to the living room and shut the door.

'What's up?' I asked. His eyes were a bit glazed and I could smell the drink on his breath.

'I've got something to show you,' he said. He took off the old suit jacket he used to wear and pulled up the sleeve of his T-shirt. He had this fresh tattoo on his right arm. It was supposed to be a heart with an arrow going through it from JACK to ZENA. It looked more like a squashed strawberry.

'What have you done that for?' I asked, laughing.

But his face was serious. 'I wanted it on,' he said. Then, 'Zena . . .' he began.

'Yeah?'

'I know it can't ever happen, I mean . . .'

'What, Jack?'

'I mean . . . if it could ever happen . . . would you marry me?'

I looked straight at him. I almost laughed, he looked so expectant and unhappy. 'Of course,' I said, and tears flooded into my eyes. But I had to bite them back. 'But it can never happen, Jack. You understand that – it can never happen.'

'I know.'

'They'd send me back rather than let me marry you. God knows what they'd do.'

JACK:
It was clear that Miriam was starting to worry about Zena's involvement with me. Where before she'd been happy to let Zena go for however long, now she restricted her trips out to just one hour. If she wasn't back within the time, Miriam would threaten, there'd be further restrictions.

Perhaps as a way round this, and perhaps just because they seemed nice guys anyway, I'd made friends with Zena's two older brothers, Kasim and Amir. Kasim was in his late twenties, a bit on the flash side, with his designer suits and his collection of exotic cars. His pride and joy was a Honda NSX, with the numberplate JAT 1, which was some kind of joke about the family's caste, the *jat-chadhuri* (which is a very high caste in Pakistan). Amir was around twenty, with the same good looks as Zena, and more interested in girls than cars.

The first time I got chatting to Kasim was when he gave me a lift. He'd passed me in his car as I trudged up the hill to my sister's. Obviously he knew I was friendly with Miriam and Zena and he pulled up beside me and wound down the window.

'Hello, mate. Going up to the street?'

'I'm on my way to my sister's.'

So he drove me up there and we exchanged a few words about what I was up to. I was trying to knock some deal in and I told him all about it. He was a successful wheeler-dealer himself, so he was interested, and we had a good chat.

Another day he passed me in another part of town altogether. That time we went for a pint together, a pint which turned into an all-night session. He was a good pool player, Kasim, and a good laugh generally. After that we used to go out together quite a bit, and sometimes Amir would come along too. On Sundays I used to show up to this football game they had in the local park. It was more of a loose kick-around than a proper game.

I used to tell Kasim about deals and scams I was involved in and he used to keep me up to speed with his own business dealings. In particular, he was very enthusiastic about the family restaurant. It had been burnt down in an arson attack. Some rowdy lads they'd thrown out of the place had come back in the small hours, poured petrol through the letter box and the whole building had gone up in flames.

Now they were doing it up and he was in charge of the refurbishment. He was going to have this carpeting, that furniture in the bar, the staircase was going to come down here, it would seat so many people . . . He was determined that it was going to be the best Indian restaurant in the city.

One time they even invited me to a cousin's wedding. Truly, I had never seen anything like it before in my life. There were over two thousand people there, in this huge hall, and the majority of them were family. The men and the women were separated by a long curtain. On one side they had tables where the guys ate, on the other where the women ate. I found that totally incredible. I was sitting there eating with the men and Kasim came up to me, laughing, waving a video camera. 'Well,' he said, 'you weren't hard to spot in this crowd, were you?' I was the only white person there.

At the end of November they offered me a job, working in their bar. I knew they were just looking for someone temporary to help them over the Christmas rush and that after that they'd get one of their relatives in. The money was terrible: I'd work from six in the evening till four in the morning for a tenner. But our friendship gave me the perfect cover for seeing Zena, so it worked both ways. If they thought they could take liberties with me I'd let them think that.

They had no idea of my involvement with their sister, of course. As I got friendlier with the pair of them I kept thinking that I ought to come clean about what was going on. It's odd to think it now, but I genuinely felt bad about it. Kasim in particular had become a good mate – I enjoyed his company – and here I was going behind his back to see his sister.

'Don't you think I should just say something?' I said to Miriam, on more than one occasion. 'For God's sake,' she'd reply, 'don't say anything. You don't understand about this, they'd go crazy.'

Zena used to tell me, too, about how serious it would be if we were ever discovered. But I always used to think to myself, I'm quite sincere here, it's not as if I'm trying to use her or take advantage of her.

The other point was: it wasn't as if they were pure as the driven snow themselves. Even after all that's happened, I don't think it's fair to go into details about this. Some things are private and personal, and Kasim was certainly never the sort of bloke to make casual conquests and brag about them the next day. But I'll say, in the context of all that followed, 'Let he who is without sin cast the first stone.'

So more than once I was on the verge of blurting out something to them. 'Look, I'm madly in love with your sister. Surely there's some way round this arranged marriage thing, some way I can marry her instead of this Bilal. I love her, my intentions are entirely honourable, I've got the greatest respect for your family and religion, surely it's possible.'

One night it was brought home to me how lucky it was that I'd taken Miriam's advice. We'd been late at the restaurant and then out to a club and as we pulled up outside the front door of their house Amir said to Kasim, 'Oh, by the way, did I tell you that so-and-so was seen at a Bhangra do with so-and-so? She's intended for what's-it, isn't she?'

It was as if someone had given Kasim a potion. I watched in amazement as he just – and this is the only word for it – erupted. 'What did you say?' And then Amir geed himself up into a frenzy too. 'Where does he go?' 'What car does he drive?' 'How can we get him and sort him out?' 'Right!' they were shouting. 'We'll go and find him, we'll get him in the car . . .' They were going to beat him up good and proper and leave him for dead.

I was sitting in the back of the car watching their contorted faces like you might watch the TV with the sound turned down. It just seemed unreal. Christ, I was thinking, this is an *Asian* guy they're talking about, a fellow Muslim. They didn't even know for definite that he was seeing this woman. Only then, I think, did the seriousness of what I'd got myself into dawn on me.

As Christmas approached Miriam was clearly starting to panic. She began to make things harder and harder for Zena and me. First she put a stop to Zena's visits to me. Then she was repeatedly telling her to break it off. Then she stopped allowing me inside their house. Then she started timing Zena's trips out, even to the local shops, and simultaneously showered her with expensive gifts, as if to remind her what she stood to lose if she carried on with it. We got to the point where we were communicating by notes dropped from Zena's bedroom window.

I'd phone in the morning at an hour when I knew Miriam would be taking Mina to nursery and Zena would give me a time to walk under her window, say 7 p.m. It was the gable end of the house, on the main road, so nobody in her family would see me as I strolled under the streetlamp and looked up to see her little face in half-silhouette above. Then she'd chuck me down a note, which I'd sometimes catch before it even hit the deck.

Now, in desperation, Miriam started threatening to tell Zena's dad. I knew that if he found out we'd be finished. Zena would be back in Pakistan and married before she knew it, and what chance would I have, hunting through an Islamic country for a woman who was someone else's wife? I might as well have slit my own throat.

It was at this point that Zena and I realized that if we wanted to be together we were almost certainly going to have to make a break for it. And soon. Zena had now discovered that her passport had been removed from the family pile and hidden.

But I've never been one not to explore all the options. So in the New Year I tried to see if there was any way we could get official help for our predicament. I'd seen how the brothers had reacted – the threat was real enough. But this was England 1993, not Kashmir 1793. Surely there must be a way we could resolve this? A court, or a government body, or a charity that could mediate?

My first port of call was the probationary department, a place I'd obviously been before. I was shown into a room in which sat a white-haired old dear who looked as if she'd been sitting there since the last war. I put my predicament to her hypothetically. 'Look,' I said, 'I've got this friend who's in this situation with this Asian woman . . .'

'Oh,' she replied when I'd finished, '*I've* got a lovely Asian colleague. Maybe he could help you.' That was the last thing I needed. Zena had already warned me that Asian people who worked for the social services might feel bound to let the family know in a case like this. It had happened before with problems that involved Asian families.

The old lady was insistent, so when this Asian colleague of hers turned up from down the corridor I told him the story, repeating of course that it was my imaginary mate who was in trouble. The man was from down south, so I felt a bit less nervous. 'Oh no,' he said, 'you've got it all wrong about the Asian community. She'll get a few slaps off the father and that'll be that. Tell your friend he'll probably end up sitting round a table talking about it.'

Things were clearly different where he came from. I'd heard enough from Miriam and Zena, and seen enough of Kasim's and Amir's reactions, not to trust in this comforting scenario.

Next I tried social services. I made an appointment to see a duty social worker and put the problem to him, again hypothetically. He was white, this man, but I knew I couldn't be too careful, even if he wasn't taken in. His advice was hardly what you'd expect from a professional. 'If I was your mate,' he said, 'I'd tell him to get as much money together as he can, and get on a train and just run for it.'

I knew then that there was absolutely nobody out there who could help us.

4

ZENA:

It was hard for us to work out our escape plan, as we were rarely able to meet any more. Things had got to the point where Miriam was timing my trips to the shops.

Now, on a grey and freezing January afternoon, she had agreed to let us meet, one final time, while my father was out at the mosque. The idea was that I should explain to Jack, once and for all, why I had to break it off. But when she'd shut the door behind us and we were alone together on the sofa in our front room, we just looked at each other and knew we had to run away. Not just talk about running away, as we'd been doing for weeks, but actually set a date.

So rather than saying our goodbyes, we plotted our escape. We decided to meet at the central train station at eleven o'clock on the following Friday morning. This was a time when I knew Miriam would be out picking up Mina from morning nursery, and my father and brothers, after the night shift at our restaurant, would still be asleep. The plan was that we'd get on the first available train and just go.

It was both terrifying and exciting, having finally set a time. As we sat there on the big curved sofa, in that comfortable room where I had spent such a happy child-hood and adolescence, we talked in low voices about how we'd survive once we'd made a break for it. We'd find another town to settle in, Jack would look for work, then we'd try to organize ourselves a flat and get married. It would be hard to start with, and we'd have to keep our heads down, but we'd be together at last.

Jack left, and I told my sister I'd finished with him. Then I ran upstairs to my little bedroom on the top floor, locked the door and started to plan what I was going to take with me. From all the bits and bats I'd accumulated over twenty-one years I had to sort out only what I could carry with two hands. It wasn't going to be an easy task.

By the Friday morning I'd worked out everything to a tee. Miriam had arranged to go over to her friend's – on the way to the nursery – at 10.30, so I'd booked the taxi for 10.35. My favourite old Derek was going to pick me up from the forecourt of a furniture warehouse round the corner. From there it was a ten-minute drive to the station and we'd be away. I'd dropped a note down to Jack the previous evening telling him I'd be there at 10.50.

I was a mess of emotions. Terrified of being caught, excited that I was finally going to be with the man I loved, but heartbroken inside to know that this was the last I was going to see of my family for a very long time. As I waved little Mina off that morning I had to struggle not to cry as she turned the corner of our street.

The clock on the mantelpiece seemed to have stopped, time was moving so slowly. I ran back upstairs to double-check my bags.

There were four of them. A big black leather sports bag full of all the Western clothes I'd ever owned: a black knitted dress that my sister had made me for my twenty-first, a coat cardigan, a beautiful black velvet evening dress that I'd actually worn on that birthday evening, and two black bodysuits.

Then there was a little sports rucksack, fluorescent yellow and purple, and an old blue bag I'd got free from Yorkshire Bank, which I'd crammed full of personal stuff: underwear, toiletries and perfume, photographs, books and even some Forever Friends candles my sister had given me that I couldn't bear to part with.

The fourth bag was full of shoes! My Ballys and Renatas and Roland Cartiers, including a special pair I'd put aside for my wedding day (wherever and whenever that would be). I'd always loved beautiful shoes: they were one way to keep up with the fashions while wearing traditional dress. You see some Asian girls wearing their *shalwar-kameez* with pink socks and plain white shoes with little block heels. You'd never catch me dead in gear like that.

I was just riffling through all this lot again when I heard a knock at the front door and then the high-pitched laugh of my sister's friend. On this day of all days she'd decided to come over to *our* house for a change! I slumped down on the top stair, my face in my hands, in a complete panic.

Come on, I told myself, stay calm, they'll probably go out in a moment. So I hurried down to say hello, praying that Miriam would suggest they leave before they disturbed my father. There they were, chatting and laughing away, and there was I, my stomach in knots, worrying about Jack waiting at the station for me. What would he think if I didn't turn up?

Then I heard a door creak open upstairs. My father had woken up. 'Can't you girls keep the noise down?' he shouted down in his familiar jovial way. I could feel tears welling up, but I knew I mustn't show my anxiety now. Miriam knew me so well she'd pick up on anything amiss. I just had to stay calm.

Just after eleven the phone rang. I heard my dad pick it up, and then the click a few moments later as he put it down. Jack must have been silent and Dad must have thought it was a heavy breather or a wrong number.

My head was in a spin. I had to get hold of Jack and tell him what had happened. Perhaps he'd think I'd changed my mind at the last minute. Or that I'd been caught, that at this very moment my father and brothers were quizzing me as to who I'd been planning to run away with. Maybe he'd turn up at the house. Maybe he'd even go to the police, fearful for his life. He knew that if my family had found out they'd have sent me straight back to Pakistan. Then they'd have gone looking for him.

I sat on my bed and tried to think straight. We had two houses, the one we lived in and our old house at the far end of the street, which Kasim was currently staying in and which was being done up ready for us to move back into. I decided that when Dad went out to his daily prayers at lunchtime I'd pretend to my sister that I was moving stuff from my present bedroom to my new bedroom in the other house.

As soon as Dad left I went backwards and forwards a few times with boxes of books so she wouldn't be suspicious. Then, telling her that I was going to be over there sorting things out for an hour or so, I half walked, half ran down to the cab rank and found Derek.

As we cut through the city centre and up the hill to Jack's mother's house my nerves were in tatters. As well as all my worries about Jack, I was terrified that Miriam would go up to our new house, find I wasn't there, run back to my bedroom, see my packed bags and raise the alarm.

I fell through Jack's mum's door in tears. 'What happened?' she asked as she hugged me. She, at least, knew we were going.

'Where's Jack? Where's Jack?' I was crying. I was in a dreadful state. Jack's mum calmed me down. Jack had come back from the station and had gone out for a pint. He was disappointed, she said, uncertain what was going on, but not panicking.

'If he comes back,' I said, before running back to the waiting cab, 'tell him everything's all right.' I explained about my father waking up and then I was off, on a hurried tour of Jack's favourite pubs. Despite his mother's reassurance, I was still desperate to catch up with him before he did anything that might wreck our plans.

I sat outside in the cab while Derek went into those places for me, bless him. But we couldn't find him. There was nothing for it but to go back home.

JACK:

While Zena was out looking for me, unknown to her I'd actually rung her house. She'd told me before that her dad went to the mosque at two o'clock on a Friday, so I took a chance that Miriam would pick up the phone.

She did, and from the tone of her voice I immediately realized that everything was all right. 'Zena's round at the other house,' she said. 'She's just moving some books.' She was very curt with me, but there was no panic there whatsoever. So I assumed that for one reason or another Zena just hadn't been able to make it. But she clearly hadn't been discovered and that was the main thing.

Back at my mother's I found out of course what had happened. Then that Zena had gone off looking for me in my usual haunts. So at five o'clock, when I knew her dad and brothers would be off to work at the restaurant, I rang again. This time Zena answered.

'Oh, Jack, thank God you called. Are you OK?'

'I'm fine, love. Everything all right there?'

'Yeah. Nobody's realized anything.'

'So what are we going to do now?'

'Can you come up?'

'Of course I can. When's best?'

'Miriam's going out to a dinner party tonight. Come up about seven. The coast should be clear then.'

I have to admit I'd had a couple to drink by the time I got up to Zena's. There'd been all this build-up, and now I didn't know what the hell was happening. Whether we were ever going to go. Whether Zena had really had second thoughts. Or what.

I'd psyched myself up for the road and said final good-byes to my mother and brother and sisters. Mum had recently got over a long illness with cancer and had only just been told she was clear from the chemotherapy treatment she'd been receiving. It hadn't been at all easy saying, 'Look, I'm off.'

When I got up to the house at seven who was still there

but Miriam – Wicked Witch of the West! Seeing me turning up again she was furious. She thought she'd got rid of me, three days before.

She let me in with a brisk nod. She didn't look happy at all. Then she followed me into the living room where Zena was waiting on their big curved black sofa.

'Right!' she said, pointing at her watch. 'This time it's really the end. I'm going to give you ten minutes to say your goodbyes, and that's it. Finished.'

Looking back, I do feel a bit sorry for Miriam. She must have been thinking to herself, 'God, what a mistake I made ever letting them even start seeing each other.' I think she knew how strong the bond had become between us by then.

When Miriam had gone Zena told me that she didn't know what she was going to do. I was still desperate to get away. But the last thing I wanted to do was put any pressure on her. It was such a huge upheaval for her, leaving her family behind like this, for ever. So I had decided I'd just try and be calm, let her know I was still there for her, still loved her, would come with her if and when she was ready. I didn't want her freaking out or doing anything rash.

I told her that everything was cool, I'd keep on popping up to see her. We also came up with this plan that if it looked at all as if they might try and whisk her suddenly back to Pakistan she would stick up these big luminous stars she had on the window of her bedroom. We agreed that if I saw them up there I'd come and get her no matter what.

Now Zena just sat there sobbing. Then Miriam came back in and said, 'You'll have to go now, Jack.'

'Give us one more minute,' Zena said. Then, when Miriam had gone, she closed her eyes and asked me to kiss her.

'Just go,' she said, the tears pouring down her face.

'It'll be all right, love,' I said. 'We'll get away one day.'

'Goodbye, Jack,' she murmured, her eyes still closed. I kissed her on the lips and backed off.

I paced slowly down the hill to the city centre. People were on their way home from work or dressed up ready for an evening out, all lost in their own little worlds. There were workmen on high ladders taking down the Christmas lights and decorations. As I watched them I thought, God only knows where I'll be when they go back up again.

I stopped off for a pint in a pub called the Three Heads. Appropriate, it seemed to me. I had enough running through my mind to fill three heads.

We hadn't made it that day. Would we ever? I had no doubts that Zena loved me, but I also knew that it was an awful lot to ask of her, to leave not just her home and family but her whole lifestyle, her whole Asian identity, for a precarious life on the run with me. We had talked about getting to another city, finding a job and saving the deposit to get a flat together, then the licence fee so we could get married – but when she sat down and thought about it all again, with her sister right beside her pouring venom into her ears, would she really want to go? On balance, I doubted it. And that goodbye she'd given me had sounded horribly final.

I left the warmth of the pub and decided to go up to my own area, have a pint or two, get a pizza and crash out at my mother's place. I didn't want to be alone in my flat in a mood like this.

Ma made us a pot of tea and we sat in that little front room of hers and talked it all over. About what might happen, what I could do, all the options. Little did I realize then that that was the last time we'd ever sit there together on that big brown corner sofa of hers, with the bookshelf between us, the little Beatrix Potter ornaments on the table under the lamp, the framed photographs of her grandchildren all around her. Now in her late fifties, Ma's auburn hair had faded to corn-gold heavily streaked with grey.

The hard life she'd had, her long battle with cancer, was written in every line on her face.

'At least you know Zena's OK, love,' she was saying.

'Yeah, Ma,' I sighed. 'I suppose so.'

'I'm sure you'll be able to work something out, Jack. Sooner or later.'

Despite everything I'd told her, Ma couldn't believe that Zena's family really would go ahead and force her to marry someone she barely knew, if I was there and it was clear she loved me.

The following morning I was lying there on the couch when I heard this tap-tap-tapping on the window. My first thought was that it was my brother Ryan's young son Simon. He used to work mucking out at a nearby stables and would often come early to the house.

'What d'you want?' I grunted. Then I heard Zena's familiar voice (I've often said she sounds like the girl from the Boddington's advert, her North Country accent is so strong). 'Let me in, it's me. Let me in, it's me.' I thought: *No, it can't be.*

I jumped off the couch and ran through to open the front door and there she was, just standing there in this massive cream Aran sweater and blue jeans with a pile of bags around her that wouldn't have looked out of place at Heathrow. The first thing that went through my head was, She's done it.

I didn't even stop to hug her. I just pulled these four bags quickly inside.

'Right,' I said, 'you sit down there. I'm going upstairs to get a wash, then I'm going to get us a lift.' I didn't know where, I didn't know who would drive us, I just knew that my heart was thumping and we were off. My mother had woken up by this time. When she came downstairs and saw those bags she knew exactly what was happening.

I'm not sure that the reality of it all hit me at the time. I ran upstairs to the bathroom almost in a daze. My mother had this big mirror in front of the sink. I remember I was leaning over, chucking water on my face to wake myself up and I just looked into it, for several long seconds. Part of me was thinking: *How the fuck did she get out?* I was absolutely stunned that she'd actually done it. Less than twenty-four hours ago I'd walked out of that train station thinking it was all over. Now she was here, we were going, and I was forcing myself to psych back into that running-away mode. I looked at myself and I all but spoke the words, 'Jack – your life is never ever going to be the same again.'

Downstairs my mother was panicking. 'They're going to turn up here now!' she was shouting. 'They're going to come after you here.'

'Calm down, Ma,' I said. 'They won't come here, will they, Zena?'

'No, Mum,' Zena replied (she used to call our mother 'Mum'). 'They might go round to Jenny's but they won't come here, I promise you.'

'Are you sure?'

'No, Ma, they won't,' I repeated. 'They could go to our sister's and they could go to the flat but they won't come here.' I couldn't see Kasim or Amir bothering with her. They knew how ill she'd been, that she was just a frail old lady, living on her own.

In any case, the brothers wouldn't even know it was me Zena had run away with. As far as they were concerned I was just a mate who had worked in their restaurant. Would Miriam tell them? She would hardly want them to find out she had known about us all along – and she was the only link.

But we had no time to stop and speculate, we had to get moving. Which meant getting to a train station straight away. And not City Central. If any of them had woken up already and discovered Zena had gone that was the first place they'd look. So I decided we'd head to this little suburban station on the outskirts. It wasn't far, but no one would surely ever think of following us there.

I knew this guy Ted who lived over the street. I ran over and banged him up. 'I've got to do a runner,' I said. 'Can't explain now but I need a lift to the station.' He knew I had a bit of a past so he didn't question it. He just rubbed his eyes, yawned and said, 'Give us two minutes to get the keys.'

As we were leaving, Ma came out. 'Don't take all those bags,' she said. 'Leave them here. The fuss'll die down in a couple of days and you can come back for them.' She really didn't have any idea quite how seriously the Asian community would react to a situation like this.

'It's OK, Mum,' Zena said. 'I'll manage them. I don't think we'll be able to get back up.'

I really don't know whether I did this to try to reassure Ma or because I half hoped she was right. But I decided to leave my bag – or, rather, binliner – behind. I only had a couple of old shirts and a spare pair of jeans in there anyway.

By this time Ted was revving up his car – a red Sierra. I told Zena to get into the back and lie down on the seat, just in case her brothers did suddenly come racing round the corner into the street. I gave my mother a quick final hug. 'Go up to Ryan's,' I said, because she hadn't got a phone at the time. 'We'll contact you there, let you know we're OK.'

As we sped off I looked round. She was walking up the pavement to the yard area where all the bins were kept. She was crying. That was my last view of her, crying as she walked up after us.

5

JACK:

We arrived at this tiny suburban rail station. We didn't have a clue what trains went from there. All we knew was that we had to get as far away from our city as quickly as we could.

We unloaded the bags and Ted shook us by the hand and wished us luck. He wouldn't accept a penny for petrol. 'I know you're going to need everything you've got,' he said with a grin. We had just over a hundred quid between us.

So there we were, not a train in sight, stamping our feet on this empty platform in the January cold. It was absolutely freezing, the coldest day we'd yet had, but we were both on a complete high. It was like being chased by the Old Bill, as if someone had got a syringe full of adrenalin and just gone *voomf* – straight into you. Neither of us could believe what was happening. That we were together – and this was it! We were going to make a go of it.

The next thing we knew, there was a train approaching. The sign on the front of the engine read 'Huddersfield'.

'This'll do for starters,' I said to Zena. Anything to get us away. So we piled the bags on.

Once we'd got moving, and were sitting back recovering our breath and watching the rows and rows of houses and gardens slipping away from us through the steamed-up windows, we rounded the corner past the football stadium and it suddenly seemed as if we were heading back into town. Oh, Christ, I was thinking, what if this cuts through the city centre and stops there? Because obviously when the brothers woke up and found Zena had gone, the first place they were going to go looking was the main station. They could be lined up on the platform waiting for us right now.

By the time the ticket inspector came round I'd managed to get us both into a complete panic.

'Does this go through City Central?' I asked.

'No, straight to Huddersfield.' You could have heard my sigh of relief in the next carriage.

When we got into Huddersfield obviously the first thing to do was to put some distance between ourselves and the station. So we lugged these bags up the hill to the town centre. It seemed as if Zena had brought her entire earthly possessions with her. There was one bag with about twenty pairs of shoes in it.

We urgently needed to find a place to stay. Not just for the night – I was extremely nervous about us being out on the streets together in daylight. We were such a conspicuous sight, this mixed-race couple in long coats trailing round four heavy bags. There are plenty of Asians in Huddersfield and, as I knew from that time I'd attended her cousin's wedding with her brothers, Zena had relatives all over the UK. So as soon as it was opening time we headed into this pub. Quite apart from the bitter cold outside, I needed a pint just to calm me down. It was one of those big old-fashioned ale houses, full of quaint signs from the 1930s advertising Bovril and Cadbury's. EXITS TO ALL ROOMS said another with a big arrow at one end of the bar.

'We can stop here with any luck,' I said to Zena, nodding at this sign. She was still over-excited and laughed hysterically at every suggestion I made. I knew it was only nerves, but in the jumpy state I was in it was starting to irritate me a little.

At the back of my mind I was thinking, We're best off in a pub B and B because if they do work out which way we've gone and catch up with us, there'll be plenty of people around. If a fight's going to break out, it'll be within the confines of the bar. The landlord'll be worried about his property and the police'll respond more quickly than they would if we were just jumped on in the street. This landlord didn't look like the sort you'd mess with either. He had the build of an ex-rugger player and so many tattoos on his arms he was a walking art gallery.

So we signed in – God knows what as, Mr and Mrs Smith, probably – and this landlord showed us to a room two floors up an old oak staircase. It was pretty shabby, with peeling flowered wallpaper and paintwork that had gone a nicotine brown with age. The narrow double divan was covered with a green candlewick quilt that looked as if it had definitely seen better days. But at least we were safely off the streets.

The first thing I did was check our exits. Six feet below our window was one of those flat gravelled roofs – it was above the back bar of the pub. Beyond, you could have dropped down into the private car park, which was surrounded by a high brick wall. That would be our way out, I decided, if it came to it.

We locked the door, jammed this wicker chair up under the handle, and crashed out for the afternoon. We didn't sleep, just lay on the quilt in our coats staring blankly at the TV, trying to take our minds off where we were, what we'd done. The adrenalin had gone now and a new, more realistic mood had set in. Zena had suddenly become like a zombie, barely registering what I said to her. She'd concentrate for a moment, then just seem to drift off into her own thoughts. She's in shock, I told myself, she'll come out of it.

Around five o'clock I decided to go downstairs and use the phone. I was desperate to find out what had happened at home, what the reaction had been when they'd discovered she'd gone missing. So I rang Jenny's house. My brother-in-law Dan picked it up.

'It's me,' I said. 'Jack.'

'You've fucking gone and done it now, a'n't you!' he was shouting at me. 'They're running up and down the fucking street. They're screaming and yelling. There's cars shooting all over the place. The whole place is full of cars —'

'For Christ's sake, calm down,' I interrupted. 'Put my sister on, I need to talk to my sister.'

Jenny came on. 'Are you all right?' she asked. She was the same kind, sympathetic sister as ever.

'We're fine,' I told her. 'We're out of the area, I can't say where we are, but we're fine. I just need to know what's going on.'

She repeated what Dan had said. All hell had broken loose. 'Then Miriam's been running up and down the street, yelling her head off and carrying on like a banshee.'

'Have they been round to yours yet?' I asked. They hadn't. Nor had they been to our mother's. That's something, I thought with relief. 'Right,' I said, 'tell Ma we're OK. I'll ring you later and tell you what our plans are.' I had absolutely no idea what our plans were.

We'd had to run away because I knew that if we didn't that was it: I'd have lost her. But now we'd gone I was starting to realize this was a complete leap into the dark. Of course I had a hope that after a couple of months things might cool down, that once we were legally married they'd accept us. But for the time being we were just out there: living on our nerves from minute to minute.

Zena:
Sitting on the edge of the bed, upstairs in that dingy little room, I could feel my whole body trembling. My stomach was in knots, not knowing how they would have taken our disappearance back home.

I could visualize the scene of Miriam coming down to the kitchen and finding the window open. Her first reaction would have been to run upstairs to my bedroom, to find my bed empty and half the stuff in my room gone.

What must she have thought? That I'd betrayed her, destroyed the trust of years of sisterly friendship? And how would she have broken the news to my dad? She'd have woken him straight away, for sure. But what would she have told him? All she knew? Or would she have been too terrified of the consequences?

And what would my father and brothers do now?

My breathing had gone funny. It felt as if I was desperately gasping for air. I squatted down on the carpet and tried to control myself with some breathing exercises from the yoga I'd always done regularly at home.

The excitement of the escape had worn off now. This room had cost us almost forty pounds for one night. If we paid for a second we'd have barely ten pounds left. What would we live on? I had a few gold bangles and a ring I could sell, but how long would that last? Then where would we go?

Less than twenty-four hours before, I'd been sobbing on my bed after my row with Miriam. The choices had looked stark: go now or lose Jack for good. Before you know it you'll be married to Bilal and that'll be that – a life of lovelessness and rows and drudgery stretching out for ever. Though at the back of my mind had been a mad hope that one day my family might accept Jack, I'd acted entirely on impulse. I had no clear idea where we'd go, what we'd live off, how we'd find work and survive.

Eventually Jack came back up and told me everything Jenny had said. Well, I thought, at least they haven't been round to hers and caused a scene, or gone tearing up to his mum's.

We sat there side by side on the divan and tried to work out what to do next, though half the time I couldn't take in what Jack was saying. It was almost as if his voice wasn't in the room with me. It was in the background, far away. I could hear it rising, as he got irritated because I wasn't replying. But I felt as if I was frozen to the edge of the bed. I couldn't move. It had just hit me quite what I'd done. I'd left my family. I'd known they'd go crazy, but now they *were* going crazy. Miriam was screaming up and down the street like a banshee, Jenny had said. If they caught up with us they'd kill us. *What had I done?*

There was no way I could talk directly to them that night. I knew I would have got nothing but a load of abuse if I'd rung them at home. So we decided to leave a message on this homeless people's service that I'd read about in the local paper. You left a message on an answerphone and they relayed it to your family.

I didn't say much, just the home phone number and something like, 'If you could tell my sister Miriam that I'm OK.' Then we went out together and got a bag of chips to eat.

It was dark now, but we were still in a total panic. We were constantly looking at cars, at people, checking the faces of everybody who passed us. We were terrified that somebody was going to spot us, *had* spotted us, was already phoning to report where we were.

When we'd finished our chips, upstairs in our room with the telly on, Jack suddenly decided that if I wasn't going to, he'd ring my family direct. 'We're going to have to deal with them sooner or later,' he said. So he left me on the bed and went downstairs and phoned them.

JACK:
As I went down to the phone I was trying to think how I could word it.

'Hello, it's me.' Or, 'Hello, I'm ringing up to see if you're all OK.' Whatever I said was going to sound bloody stupid. Obviously, I knew from my sister that the shit had really hit the fan. But I had to find out how they were taking it. Get it from the horse's mouth.

Well, I thought, as I stood there in the little booth with

a stack of ten p's, it's got to be done. So I dialled the number.

'Hello,' came Miriam's voice.

'It's me,' I said. 'Jack.'

She was instantly screaming at me. 'Where've you fucking got to? . . . What's fucking going on? . . . What's fucking happening?' All that sort of thing. I'd never heard her talk like that before.

'Calm down, Miriam,' I said. 'We're not going to get anywhere like this, so calm down. I'm just ringing to let you know that Zena's OK. She's fine, she's with me. Our plans are that we're going to get married. And we're more than willing to sit down and try and talk this through—'

'It's a bit bloody late for that,' Miriam cut in. 'You can tell Zena that her dad's gone and had a heart attack.'

Oh shit no, I thought. I can't hide this from her. She's got to know.

So I asked Miriam which hospital he was in. 'OK,' I said, 'we'll get back to you.' I slammed the phone down and ran back up to Zena.

When I told her the news I was expecting her to shout or scream or break down or something. But she just sat there on the carpet with these big blank eyes. Then she got up. 'Right,' she said slowly, 'the first thing we've got to do is ring that hospital and check this out.'

Looking back on it now, it's clear that though Zena was in shock she was the one seeing things clearly. But to me at that moment it seemed as if the news hadn't impinged properly at all. She was so calm, I wondered if she was cracking up.

We went downstairs together, I got another pile of tenpence coins from the barman and we rang first the place Miriam had named and then all the hospitals her father could possibly be in – every single one within our city's area.

There was nobody registered under his name in any of them.

We sat side by side on the bed upstairs and decided that it had to be a con. They were obviously doing it to get back at her, or to try and trick her into going home. Nonetheless, just to make sure, we went back down again and rang all the hospitals a second time. No, there was no record of any Mohammed Chadhaury coming in with cardiac problems or anything else.

ZENA:
When Jack ran in and told me that Dad had had a heart attack it didn't properly sink in at first. My immediate thought was, It's my fault. If he dies they'll blame me for it. Then I was thinking, No, it can't have happened, it's a hoax, we've got to phone the hospital, check if he really is there.

After we'd phoned all the hospitals in the area twice I just knew they'd made it up. They were trying to get me to go running home. It was only our first day away and already my family had resorted to lies and trickery.

Neither of us slept that night. Apart from our trip to Pakistan, I'd never been away from home before, and obviously in part it was the strangeness of the environment, this horrible little room with its scrappy MFI furniture and dirty net curtains, so different from the comfort and cleanliness I'd known before.

It had also been my first day in Western clothes. We attracted enough attention just by walking together, and wearing traditional gear would have only made it worse. Now in this pair of Amir's old jeans and one of his striped shirts I felt very strange indeed.

But above all we were convinced that they were bound to catch up with us. Somebody would see us, we thought, somebody would report it back. Or they could easily have worked out that we'd run from that little suburban station, and then the time, and from that where the train had taken us. Or else they would have traced one of our phone calls.

Every time we phoned home we made certain the call lasted less than three minutes. (This was before you could dial 1471, but that didn't stop us worrying.)

So we lay awake together, fully dressed on top of the quilt with our coats thrown over us. Jack had this long black trenchcoat and I had a shorter khaki one. We kept the lights on. If somebody had seen us in town and had followed us and phoned my family, and suddenly there was a hammering at that door, we didn't want to be jumping out of bed in total darkness.

'Honey,' I said to Jack as we lay there, 'just stroke my head, love.' I closed my eyes and tried to forget where we were.

He just kept talking, telling me that he loved me, that it would be all right, we were going to get far away and find a nice place to live. Then he went off into the fantasies we'd sometimes had on our walks in the park, about how the house we'd finally settle in would be furnished, what it would look like . . .

It made me feel better, but we were still both as tense as cats. At first we could hear the noise of the cars coming and going in the street, and the chatter and music of a Saturday night coming up from the bar below, but when that had died away the silence seemed deathly. Every banging door, every footstep outside made us jump. *It's them, they're here, they've found us.*

The next morning, drained of energy, we decided we'd stay put for the Sunday night too. We sat in our little room all day going over and over our situation, trying to work out what would be best, where to run from here, where would be safest. I spent an hour or two rearranging the stuff in my bags. Underneath that heavy khaki coat the Aran sweater was far too hot when we were walking, even though it was January; so that got rolled up and put away.

At dusk we headed outside, went for a long walk round those narrow, dark back alleys of central Huddersfield that make you feel almost as if you're in Victorian times. Even though it was dark we were constantly looking over our shoulders.

'Don't act like you're a stranger,' Jack kept telling me. 'Just act normally, as if we live here, as if we're just going to our local shop.' Then: 'Don't fidget,' he'd say, if we were sitting in the bar of the pub or at a table in a café. But I was still very agitated, I found it very hard. And I kept swinging into this mad mood where I was laughing hysterically at the slightest thing.

JACK:
We went out that evening to pick up some chips. When we got back to the pub I decided I was going to ring the Chadhaurys again. I wanted them to know that we hadn't fallen for their stupid hoax.

It was Miriam who answered.

'I'm just ringing to tell you that we've phoned round all the hospitals,' I said, 'and there's no Mr Mohammed Chadhaury in any of them. I know you're not happy with what's happened, but you shocked Zena out of her wits with that news.'

It wasn't a very nice way to treat your own sister, I went on, expecting Miriam would insist the story was true. But she said nothing and suddenly Kasim came on. I took it that he'd snatched the phone from his sister. He didn't even bother to mention the heart attack story.

'You're not going to get far, Jack,' he said, and I was immediately shocked by the new cold, matter-of-fact tone in his voice. It was as if I was speaking to another person, not the charming, humorous Kasim I'd been mates with before. 'We've got a bounty hunter out looking for you,' he went on. 'I'm selling my cars and I'm going to make it my life's mission to find you. And when we do find you I'm going to make sure you're killed. Slowly. You're both going to end up in binliners. Not one, but several. And when that happens we'll have stone-clad alibis. So you might as well just bring her back and leave it at that.'

'I'm not bringing her back,' I replied as calmly as I could. I was trying desperately to keep the panic out of my voice. I didn't want him to know how badly he'd got to me. 'I love her, we're going to get married, and you've got to accept this.'

'It doesn't matter how long it takes,' Kasim continued. 'Months or years, we'll find you in the end. You're a walking corpse, mate.'

He put the phone down with a click, and I saw that the receiver was shaking in my hand. The thing that had made me realize he was completely in earnest was this talk of selling his cars. He was a shrewd businessman, Kasim, and over the years he'd accumulated a fair bit of money. The cars he'd spent most of it on were the love of his life.

I ran back upstairs to Zena and told her what he'd said. 'Is it possible?' I asked. 'Does this bounty hunter exist?'

'Oh yeah,' she replied. 'Without a doubt. If they say they're going to get him, they'll already have hired him.'

This bounty hunter is famous, apparently, within the Asian community. The way it works is that he gets paid a sum in advance for finding a runaway girl, and he doesn't get settlement till he's found her. He uses his own network, the Asian network that stretches across Britain like a web, through restaurateurs, shopkeepers, minicab drivers and so on. He carries photographs and videos, and just goes from city to city, asking if people have seen the girls he's looking for. If they can't help immediately he'll ask them to ring him if they hear anything. And everybody he sees will be happy to co-operate, because no one wants these young women running away from their arranged marriages. It could be their daughter next.

He's not licensed as a private detective, or as anything else. But there's no way the police can pick him up for what he's doing, because although he's well known in the Asian community if he was asked by someone in authority about what he does he would just deny it.

We were panicked enough, anyway. The thought of this bounty hunter didn't exactly help our state of mind. Huddersfield was full of Asian faces. Who knew how quickly this fellow worked?

Zena still had her four heavy bags. As we sat upstairs in our room that evening I told her that we were going to have to offload some of her stuff. As well as the shoes and clothes, she'd brought face cream and hand cream and perfume and you name it – everything but the kitchen sink.

'We've got to be realistic, love,' I said. 'We can't hump all this gear everywhere.'

So we went through them, sorting out the things she could most easily live without – a full French manicure set, for example. She hardly needed that on the run. I went downstairs and knocked on the landlord's private door.

'Look, mate,' I said. 'We've paid for our room . . .'

'I know you have . . .'

'But we're in a bit of a fix,' I said. 'Maybe your wife could use some of this gear.' There was about two hundred quid's worth of nail varnish and manicure stuff. He knew I was desperate so I only got twenty out of him for it all.

Still, that was enough to get us two train tickets on to Sheffield the next morning. As we left the B and B room I looked round at the peeling floral wallpaper and yellow-brown paintwork and under my breath said, 'Thank you', to the four walls. For keeping us safe. It may sound strange but it was something I did from then on, in every place we stopped.

Our plan was to find a pawnbroker's and try to sell some of Zena's jewellery. We eventually found what we needed at the far end of the high street.

Zena had two golden Indian bangles that were so soft they were pliable in your hands. This isn't gold, I thought, but I couldn't have been more wrong. It was, the pawnbroker told us, the finest twenty-four-carat yellow gold. We got nearly four hundred pounds for the pair of them.

'Right,' I said, as we traipsed back out on to the street,

'now we've got a bit of cash I think we should keep moving. Get right out of the area.'

We had no idea where we were going. We hurried back into the train station past this long line of cab drivers, every last one of whom seemed to be Asian. I looked up at the big destination board and saw there was a train to Scarborough. 'OK,' I said to Zena. 'We'll go to Scarborough.' Even though it was January I had some kind of crazy idea that I might be able to get casual work there.

She looked at me blankly. 'Where's Scarborough?' she said. She'd been a bit spaced-out the day before, but this made me seriously worried. Please, I thought, please, please don't go cabbage on me. If she cracked up now I knew we'd never make it.

I left her sitting in the station café with a beaker of hot coffee and the bags and hurried over to the ticket desk.

'Right,' I said. 'What's the first train out of here?'

'To where?' asked the ticket clerk.

'Anywhere.'

This threw him completely. 'Anywhere?' he repeated.

'Yeah.'

'Well, there's a train leaves in ten minutes for Cleethorpes.'

'Give us two singles to Cleethorpes, then.'

I didn't have a clue what Cleethorpes was like, whether it had a large Asian population, where it was, even. The point was that we were moving; and while we were moving we felt safe. However clever they'd been, however many people they'd asked, however good the bounty hunter was, we were, I felt, one step ahead of them.

6

JACK:
So we rattled across the wintry countryside for an hour or
so and arrived at Cleethorpes, which turned out to be a
small, scruffy-looking resort on the east coast of Yorkshire.
You certainly wouldn't pick it if you could choose anywhere in the world, and on that bleak January afternoon
it looked particularly run-down.

Just around the corner from the train station we came
upon this street full of bed and breakfasts. They all had
Vacancies signs up in the front window, but the first three
places we tried took one look at us and said they were
sorry, it was a mistake, the card shouldn't be in the
window, all of a sudden they had no vacancy.

Whether it was because Zena wasn't white, or just that
we were in such a terrible state, they didn't tell us. I had
nothing to change into, so I was still in the same jeans and
T-shirt I'd left home in on the Saturday morning. It was
now Monday night and I'd done a lot of walking, not to
mention lugging bags, so I can't have been very savoury.

On our fourth attempt we got lucky. We signed in with
the old lady who ran the place and she showed us to a
ground-floor room with a bay window and two separate
beds, one single, one double, separated by a small dresser.
We grabbed one each and just collapsed. We were both,
physically and mentally, exhausted.

That evening we went out to get something to eat. We
shared a bag of chips and walked on, round a corner and
on to the front. There was a row of amusement arcades.

To the right, the open sea. We stood together in the wind, watching the waves crashing up on to the sand. It was 1 February, and still bitterly cold.

'Let's go for a pint,' I said, as we turned to go. 'Before we go back in.'

'No, love, we've got to be careful with this money.'

'There's four hundred quid there.'

'I know, but that's all we've got.'

'Just a pint, Zena. Just to help me sleep.'

'No, love, you're not having a pint tonight.'

I gave in. I knew Zena could be stubborn as a mule but this was the first time she'd been like that with me. We strode back in silence.

ZENA:

'I'll have the double bed, then,' he said, when we got in. He was still in a right sulk about us not having stopped out for a pint. 'You can have the single.'

'No, I won't,' I said. 'I paid for the bloody room, you have the single.'

Anyway, I ended up in the double. But it was freezing cold in that room. The wind rattled at the window panes. Halfway through the night I heard Jack's voice.

'Love?'

'Yeah, what?'

'Can I come into yours? It's so bloody cold.'

'All right, then,' I said. 'Come on.' He came over and lay next to me under the quilt. We were both still fully clothed, in case we had to make a run for it.

We stayed at that bed and breakfast for two more nights, getting a cheaper rate from the landlady by not taking breakfast. Instead we found a café on the front where you could get eggs and toast with a coffee for £1.10. That did us for the day. In the evening we might share a bag of chips or a Chinese omelette. I was too tense and nervous to eat much more in any case.

We spent the days indoors, staring at the telly. Though we'd seen no Asian faces in Cleethorpes, we still felt safer indoors. Once again we barricaded the door with an arm-chair. At night we kept the lights on, just to be sure. We were so exhausted we were sleeping now, but we made sure we took it in turns, so one of us was always awake. Jack would say, 'I'll get me head down for a couple of hours,' and then when he woke it would be my turn.

JACK:

As we walked out along the beach the next evening I decided to give my brother Ryan another call. See what the crack was now. Zena and I squeezed into a kiosk at the end of the front.

His wife Linda picked up the phone. Straight away she was yelling at me, 'They've found the notes under the bed! Whatever you do, get out of Blackpool.'

'Blackpool?' I queried. Then as Zena started nudging me, I clicked. When we'd originally tried to leave on the Friday morning we'd planned to go to Blackpool. Zena had written down all the train times on a piece of paper, and when our attempt had failed she'd screwed it up and left it under her bed. So when the family had searched her bedroom the first thing they'd found was this list of train times to Blackpool. Kasim, Amir and Salim had raced down there, looking for us.

'It's OK,' I said, breathing easily for the first time since we'd left. 'It's cool. We're on the opposite side of the country. I can't say where we are, but don't worry about it.'

Then it struck me. How the hell did she know about this anyway? The brothers, Linda explained, had paid Jenny a call. 'We know where they are,' they'd said, 'for a fact. They're in Blackpool and it's only a matter of time before we have them.'

'There's another thing I've got to tell you,' Linda went on. 'They've been down to Mum's.'

'What d'you mean?' I asked, and there was a long pause. 'What's happened? Is she all right?'

They'd turned up, Linda told me, at about eleven o'clock at night. Four of them. They'd smashed my mother's windows, broken down her door, then gone in, grabbed her and pinned her up against a wall. 'We want you to be introduced to the man who's going to murder your son,' they'd said.

'Just say that again,' I said. '*What* happened?' I was numb with shock.

'Where's Mum now?' I said when she'd finished. 'Have they been charged? What's happened?'

There was a group of students living in the house next to my mother's at the time. When they'd heard the windows being smashed, they'd run out into the street, apparently, so once the brothers and their accomplice had made their threat they'd scarpered.

I stood there holding the phone in disbelief. From the days when we'd been friends, Kasim and Amir knew my mother was seriously ill, had fought a long and painful battle with cancer. They knew she was an elderly woman who lived on her own.

Ryan was so angry, Linda said, that he was ready to go up and take one of them out. He wasn't just saying that, he meant it. My head felt like it was ready to explode, but I had to stand there and say, 'He's got to stay calm. These are just their tactics.' I knew Ryan and I knew what he was like. He's volatile, and if he gets an idea like that into his head there's nothing in the world will stop him. 'Tell Mum,' I went on, 'that I'll try and get in touch with her and not to worry about us. We're fine.'

The hatred I felt just then for that family was unbelievable. I couldn't believe they would sink so low.

Zena was squashed up next to me in the phone box. 'Right,' I said to her. 'Give us your dad's phone number.'

I rang straight through and got Miriam. 'You're fucking bang out of order doing this,' I said. 'You're not looking for my mother, you're looking for me and you're looking for Zena. You're not looking for anyone else, stick to what you're doing. Because if I hear that they've been down there again, then I'm telling you, all-out war is going to break out. D'you get that? She's frail,' I went on. 'How brave are they? It takes a load of them to go down, steam into a house, put her windows through, grab hold of her. I mean, what kind of men are these?'

'I don't know what you're talking about, I don't know what you're talking about,' Miriam was protesting.

'You know *exactly* what I'm fucking talking about . . .' And I kept blowing off and blowing off. In the end I just slammed the phone down.

I suppose, deep down, I'd known that they would go down to my mother's. But because they have such respect for the elderly in their own culture, I'd foolishly thought that what they'd do was just knock on the door, say something like, 'Look, we're really concerned about our sister . . .' and take it from there. I'd never for a moment envisaged that they'd use such disgusting tactics. I was so angry that if I'd been able to get my hands on a gun I'd have been up there on the train without hesitation. I'd have blown Kasim's head straight off his fucking shoulders.

We came out of the box and my mind was reeling. 'Come on,' I said, 'let's have a drink.' We marched over the road and went straight into this pub. I got us some drinks and we sat down. When I'd calmed myself and sorted my head out a little I said to Zena, 'Look, love, this isn't directed at you. This hasn't changed anything between me and you. I love you and I know that if you could have controlled the situation this would never have happened. I'm not going to let them get in between us.'

Before we went to bed that night I went back out to the phone box and managed to get through to Jenny. 'Have you heard what's gone on?' I said.

Had she heard what was going on! She'd only had this huge crowd of Muslim women chanting in Urdu outside their front door for the best part of the previous evening. Things were getting totally out of hand.

'But you see there's nothing I can do about it from where I am,' I said.

'Did you think they'd go down to Mum's, Jack?'

'I did think they might go down, but not in a million years did I think they'd behave like that . . .'

Jenny accepted that. Then she told me about her own visit from the brothers – Kasim, Amir and Salim. Dan, my brother-in-law, has a bit of a reputation for being able to take care of himself, so they hadn't tried anything violent with him. There'd just been an angry exchange of words on the doorstep. Dan had said that he was sick and tired of them screaming up and down the street, frightening his children by sitting in their cars right outside his front window. He didn't have a clue where we were.

They shouted back at him about the bounty hunter. That he was after us, that he was on the move, tracking us down. They'd hired a private investigator, too, they told him. A white man. And they were pursuing their own lines of enquiry. It was only a matter of time before someone caught up with us.

When I put the phone down my first thought was, We can't settle here. We can stop for a night or two and recover our breath while they mess around in Blackpool. But then we've got to get back on the road.

ZENA:

I was squashed up next to Jack in the phone box and I could hear everything. The first thing that ran through my mind was that I'd promised his mum they wouldn't call on her. I felt so ashamed at what they'd done; ashamed, and then, when I thought about it more, angry.

I was also thinking about Jack's family – Karen, Ryan

and Jenny. What would they think of me now? I was privately terribly worried that this might turn them against me, that they might want to try to persuade Jack to give up on me.

When I'd heard Jack swearing at my sister I thought, Oh no, now he's going to go back up there and he and Ryan are going to go and try and sort them out. I knew that would have ended in a bloodbath. And if he'd gone back I'd have had to go too, so they'd have achieved their aims, getting us both exactly where they wanted us.

But once Jack had got over his initial fury and calmed himself down, it was clear he wasn't going to allow himself to be riled. Then he did a lovely thing: he put his arm round me and told me that whatever my brothers did, it would never change his love for me. It was as if he'd heard my thoughts, and that made me love him even more.

By the third day we felt we'd recovered enough to move on. We packed up our stuff and bought a ticket to Grimsby. We thought it would be quite a distance but we'd no sooner got our bags on to the train and sat down than Grimsby station loomed up – it was barely five miles down the coast.

'Look,' Jack said, as we got off the train, 'I'm sick of lugging all these bags around everywhere. Let's just bung them in a left-luggage place overnight while we find a place to stay. We can come back and get them in the morning.'

So we locked them up in a couple of those filing-cabinet-type platform lockers, stuffed our toothbrushes and a change of underwear in my handbag, and set off down the road into Grimsby. It was just starting to get dark, and we prayed that it wouldn't be too long before we found a B and B to take us.

This time we were in luck; the first place we saw, a pub, gave us a room. It was pretty expensive, over forty quid for the night, but at least we could get our heads down. We were both shattered. We bought some bread and John West salmon pâté to make sandwiches and, having barricaded ourselves in again, crashed out in front of the TV.

7

ZENA:

In the morning Jack got hold of the *Yellow Pages*, phoned round a few more B and Bs and found a cheaper place to stay. When we got there it was a bit of a dive – two pebble-dashed houses knocked into one right on a main road, opposite a stretch of derelict land. The landlord was a very shifty-looking character, too. The room he showed us to had two single beds and an old Victorian fireplace blocked off with unpainted hardboard. But we didn't care. The main thing was that he'd take us and it was cheap.

We got a sandwich in a pub in town and then headed back to the station to pick up our bags.

We walked round the corner on to the platform, and there were our two luggage lockers, doors swinging open, empty.

I felt sick to my stomach.

They've caught up with us! That was my first thought. Either the bounty hunter or the white private investigator. My heart raced and my hands were shaking. Then I thought: All my stuff is in those bags. Everything I have in the world, even down to photographs of my family, the last thing I have of them.

A porter came out and saw us standing there. 'Was that your luggage in there?' he asked.

'Yeah,' Jack replied. 'What's happened?'

'Oh,' he said, 'it was broken into last night. But the thief was disturbed by the transport police and he did a runner and left the bags behind. They've been taken to Grimsby main police headquarters. You'll have to pick them up from there.'

'This is all we bloody need,' Jack murmured to me under his breath. It wasn't just his criminal record that made him worried about going to a police station. There was still a warrant out for an outstanding fine from two years before. If they started making him fill in reports and checking his details this would come up on computer and then they'd arrest him and take him back home.

The stupid thing was that I'd left most of the money we'd got from the bangles in one of the bags, and what with train fares and bed and breakfasts we'd spent the rest. So we *had* to get them. And by now the British Rail transport police had turned up and were insisting on taking us over to the main Grimsby police station.

When we got there I was very nervous. But the grey-haired duty sergeant seemed friendly enough.

'So whose bags are they, then?' he asked.

'They're mine.'

'You want to look through and see if anything's missing?'

'No, no,' I said quickly. 'That'll be fine.'

'I should just check, love, if I were you.'

'No, no, it's fine, I'll sort it out when I get back to the B and B.'

He kept repeating that I should check them, and I didn't know what to say, but Jack stepped in, acting very casual, with, 'Sorry, mate, it's been a bit of a traumatic day. As you can see, our lass is upset, we'll definitely be in touch if there's anything gone missing.' And luckily this policeman just let us take them and go. As Jack said, he was glad, probably, not to have to bother with the paperwork.

When we got back to the B and B we searched the bags. I'd hidden the money, along with all my family photographs, in an envelope at the bottom of the largest black sports bag, under a strip of plastic that ran along its base.

I reached in and found nothing. 'Oh, Jack,' I gasped. It

wasn't just our money that had gone. All my perfume, a load of luxury underwear, and all the photographs, too. I burst into tears.

Of course I minded about the money, which was vital for our survival, but at that moment I actually cared more about the photographs. There'd been one of my father, and another one of my sister's little girl, Mina, and a stack of others of us all together in happier days. All gone now. It felt as if the only remaining link I had with my family had been taken away. And the personal stuff, the underwear and perfume – these were private things. That thief had rummaged through with no thought of what they meant to me. I felt violated, as if somebody had taken part of me. I cried and cried, sitting there on the floor of our bedroom in the B and B.

Jack tried to calm me. 'Look, love,' he said, sitting down beside me. 'It's happened now – they've gone. We've got to work out what we're going to do about money. We've got enough for a couple of nights' B and B and after that there's nothing, so we've got to put the other stuff to the back of our minds and concentrate on that.'

JACK:
It might seem heartless – I knew how important those photographs were to Zena because she used to bring them out and look at them every night – but at that moment I couldn't see beyond the practicalities of our survival. With the £200 gone we had enough for two more nights' B and B and then we were on the streets. It was the beginning of February – hardly the time of year to kip on the beach.

I decided I'd go downstairs to the landlord to see whether I might be able to talk him into letting us sign on for housing benefit. I pulled him into the little TV lounge and told him I'd got enough money for a couple of nights but we needed to stay longer while I looked for work.

'Is there any chance,' I asked, 'of me making a claim here?'

'Oh, that's OK,' he replied. 'No problem.'

With a rush of relief I thought, Great, we can settle here for a while and sort ourselves out. Maybe I could get a casual job, down at the docks or wherever. Then we could start saving up the £75 we needed for the marriage licence.

It was our number-one priority to get married as soon as possible. Until then, if the family did catch up with us, in their eyes Zena was still their property. She could still be taken back to Pakistan and delivered to Bilal. Once she became my wife, though, I would have rights.

And at the back of my mind, still, I hoped that once they realized we had got married they might back down a bit; not necessarily offer a full reconciliation, but at least agree to a truce.

So the next morning – it was a Friday – we headed off bright and early to the DSS to make a claim. We waited the usual hour or two in this room full of screaming kids and eventually got to fill in the necessary B1 form. Before I handed it over, I insisted on a private interview. I wanted to explain our circumstances to someone senior, to try to get an emergency grant. After the advance we'd given to our B and B landlord we had only a few pounds left.

I was also very worried about giving out our real names, addresses and National Insurance numbers. I knew that when you made a new application the computer checked back to your last entry, so the information about where we were claiming now would be available in our home town and, since there were plenty of Asians working in the DSS at home, I wanted to make sure that the whole thing would be treated in complete confidence.

Eventually we got an interview, with a senior manager, a stern lady in black spectacles. We told her everything. That we were on the run, being hunted for our lives, that this wasn't just a threat, it was reality. She listened to our story and seemed to believe us, but she nevertheless wasn't able to help us with an emergency advance. We would have to go through the normal channels, she said, and it would be ten to twelve days before we received payment.

'So what do we live on?' I asked. 'We're down to our last few pounds.'

'I'm very sorry,' she replied. 'I'd like to help, but there are official procedures and we have to stick to them.' She reassured us, though, that all our details would be treated in strictest confidence, since it was illegal to pass on information within or from the DSS.

With just a few pounds to live on, we managed to sell some Indian silver jewellery that the thief hadn't bothered with. It fetched us ten pounds, which we portioned out to cover each day until our payments were due.

The landlord, having seen copies of our housing benefit forms, let us continue to stay in the room. We'd got a cheaper rate by not taking breakfast, so for the next seven days we kept going on pot noodles and cream crackers. We'd boil up the kettle in our room, pour the water into a pot noodle, then spread it over a few cream crackers. This, together with salmon pâté sandwiches and the occasional bag of chips in the evening, became our regular diet.

All this was harder for Zena than it was for me. I'd had the odd rough patch before, been inside and so forth. But she'd never left home, and had been used to three square meals a day.

It wasn't just the going to bed hungry and the lack of home comforts. The daily stress of this situation, the constant fear we felt, was having a terrible effect on her. Already, after only a week or so, she'd lost a visible amount of weight. Her skin had a sickly pallor and was taut over her cheekbones. She had huge bags under her eyes. She looked ill.

At night we continued to leave the lights on and the door barricaded. We stuck with our pattern of sleeping in turns. Zena would have the sheets and the bedding, I'd take the quilt and either deck out on the floor or lie crossways on top of the duvet at the foot of the bed.

By day we mostly sat in front of the TV – which looked like the first colour TV ever made, as solid as a tank – half watching the endless diet of quiz shows, news programmes and Australian soaps. If someone had asked us, 'What did that man just say?' we probably wouldn't have known. We weren't really concentrating, more just staring, taking our minds off the constant drip, drip, drip of fear. What are they doing now? Where have they got to? What leads is the private investigator following? And the bounty hunter? Are there any Asian faces in Grimsby who've seen us who we haven't seen? What *haven't* we anticipated? Because I knew from experience that if something was to happen, it would come, as always, from a totally unexpected direction.

Every day as we walked into town to the DSS (our claim was taking for ever to sort out) we had to cross this narrow green metal footbridge near the railway.

'Christ,' I said to Zena, 'if they caught up with us when we were crossing this we'd be fucked.' Because the only way out would have been to jump. And either break both legs or fry on the electric rails beneath. The thought that somehow they might catch up with us there terrified me. I always hurried us over that bridge.

After a few days of the pot-noodle and cracker diet it got to the point where it did occur to me to shoplift something. But Zena would have none of it. In her religion to steal was a terrible thing. 'No,' she told me, 'we'll struggle through however hard it gets.' I thought to myself, Wait till we're down to just biscuits and water and then see where your morals are.

There was another point too. Sod's law if I *had* tried anything on I'd have got caught. And if I'd been nicked, with my record and the outstanding fine, they'd have taken me back home to jail straight away and Zena would have been left on her own in this shitty little bed and breakfast in Grimsby. With no experience of surviving outside the comfortable middle-class world she'd been used to. I wasn't prepared to risk that.

We'd been on the run for barely two weeks, but already Zena was starting to move into my world. I felt very responsible for her. Just seeing her react in the way she had to the theft of the photographs, and having to go to the police station, I realized how difficult all of this was for her. My feelings were clear-cut. But hers, with twenty-one years of loving this family that was now pursuing her with death threats, were a total muddle.

I was still wearing the clothes I'd left home in and I really must have stunk to high heaven by then. 'If I don't get out of these soon,' I joked to Zena, 'I'm going to have to have them surgically removed.' We had just enough money left for the launderette, but I had nothing to change into. 'You must have something in them bags,' I said. 'A blouse or summat I could wear.' I ended up squeezing into this black bodysuit of Zena's. I could barely breathe and looked a right prat. Zena offered to go down and do my laundry for me, but I didn't want her going out on her own. In a relatively white place like Grimsby she was so much more conspicuous than me.

ZENA:
Even though we still kept the armchair barricaded across the door at nights and took it in turns to sleep, we were on edge all the time. Grimsby, we thought, was where we might settle. At least for the time being. It was far enough from home, there were hardly any Asians, and Jack was planning to try and get a job down at the docks.

Eventually, after much to-ing and fro-ing to the dole offices, we managed to get our claims sorted out. It took us the best part of a week in the end, going back each day, waiting for hour after hour in this dirty, overcrowded room till we were finally called in to see this lady who was dealing with us. I'd been on welfare before, when my father's restaurant burnt down, but getting it sorted out had never been such a hassle as this. I think it was because we didn't have a permanent address that it all took so long.

One night we'd decided to break the monotony and step out for a drink. We'd sold a silver necklace of mine for a few quid and Jack reckoned he deserved a treat. We found this little hotel bar and after a pint or two Jack got talking to two local guys, Vince and Gary. Vince was the local amateur boxing champion and looked it, a great big brawny hulk of a man. Gary was his mate, thin and wiry, and very proud of Vince's title. After we'd all had a couple of drinks together we told them our story. They were far more shocked at our situation than the lady at the DSS had been. They insisted on giving us these two big sheath knives with leather casings that hooked on to the back of your waistband. We took to wearing these all the time, under our coats as we walked around town. At night we kept them beside us.

Now our thoughts started to turn to other practicalities. We went down to the registry office and found out the procedure for getting a three-day marriage licence. The cost was £75. Then we visited a solicitor. We wanted to find out whether there was any legal way out of our predicament. Jack had the idea that it might be possible to take out an injunction against my family to stop them harassing us.

We signed the green legal aid form and saw a young solicitor called Caroline Brown. She listened to our story. No, she told us when we'd finished, there was nothing she could do for us, the law was powerless in this situation.

'So what can we do?' we asked.

'You might as well enjoy it while you can,' she replied, 'because they're going to catch up with you sooner or later, aren't they?'

'Well,' said Jack as we got outside, 'that was reassuring.' He wasn't making light of our situation; but humour was always the way he dealt with things; it was something, he used to say, he'd inherited from his mother.

Our giro still hadn't arrived so we'd given up on pot noodles and were eking out our few remaining pounds on salmon pâté sandwiches. The worst night we had to share one sandwich – we just had no money left at all.

A young mother with three kids moved in down the hall. So we were now sharing the little bathroom at the top of the stairs, with its rickety shower and yellow-stained bath. One of the kids must have been ill as the toilet was often covered in shit and vomit, which we had to clean off. At night the mother used to go out on her own, leaving the kids locked up in their room. When I went up to the bathroom late I'd hear them shouting, 'Is that you, Mum?' My heart went out to those poor children.

It was Valentine's Day the day Jack went to the launderette. Despite the fact that we were down to nothing he came back with a Valentine's card for me. As I stood there holding it I remembered that other card I'd received a year before, which Kasim had got so furious about. What a long, long time ago that all seemed now.

I loved Jack and I didn't, in my heart, ever doubt that I'd made the right decision in leaving. But, oh, how I missed the love, comfort and security of home! The tenderness and friendship of my father and sister and brothers – not, obviously, as they were now, but as they had been before.

I missed the feminine companionship of Miriam, Henna and Elisa terribly; just having women around you, who you could talk to about personal things.

I missed the comfort of getting up in the morning and washing in my own clean bathroom with hot water in the powerful shower, and my own things around me. Of going downstairs knowing that Miriam would be there getting the breakfast ready and of knowing that the cupboard would be full of food. As I counted our last few coins to buy pot noodles or custard creams in the little supermarket we visited, I'd look round at the stacked-up aisles and think of the times when I'd casually walked through loading up my trolley with tubs of ice cream and bottles of Coke and all the little luxuries I'd taken for granted for so long. 'Money doesn't come out of a tap, you know, Zena,' my father had often told me. Now I was starting to understand what he meant.

Above all I missed the security of home: that absolute sense of safety which surrounds you like a blanket. It was the total opposite of this little boxroom at the B and B, with its window looking straight on to the bleak and impersonal main road and the wide, litter-strewn, pavement on the far side.

8

ZENA:

About half-seven on the following Monday morning there
was a loud knock on our bedroom door. We both sat
straight up on our beds, then I hopped out on to the carpet
and ran over to answer it. 'Who is it?' I asked.

'There's a phone call for you,' came the voice of our
landlord.

'Phone call!' I replied, relieved that it was only him, but
surprised too. Who, I wondered, could possibly be phoning
me here, at this time?

I went out into the corridor in my dressing gown and
took the phone. 'Is that Zena Chadhaury?' It was a man's
voice: English, neutral, nobody I recognized.

'Yeah, speaking,' I said. 'Could I ask who's calling,
please?'

'It's Mr Adams,' he replied. 'From the Unemployment
office. We'd like you to come back down here because
there's some forms you haven't filled in correctly.'

'Is that just for me?' I asked, relieved. On the Friday
afternoon, at the end of all the palaver at the DSS, we'd
given the woman who'd been dealing with us our phone
number – in case she needed further information. So I
assumed it was a colleague of hers. 'D'you want to see my
fiancé too?'

'No, it's just for yourself,' this voice answered. 'If you'd
like to come down within the hour we can get these forms
sorted out.'

I went back to our room and told Jack. He was immediately suspicious. 'That's very strange,' he said, 'them phon-

ing for you so early. The office doesn't open till half-nine.'

I did have a bit of an odd feeling about this phone call too. But for some reason my doubts were concentrated on the person who'd broken into our bags. What if he's got my name? I thought. What if he's some nutter who's kept the photos and has been following me around? What if . . . ? My imagination was running wild, but the one thing that never occurred to me was that my family had finally caught up with us, because the DSS had told us that they were a completely confidential organization. They had reassured both of us on that specific point. And how else could my brothers have known we were in Grimsby? We'd kept well clear of the few Asian faces we'd seen – in Grimsby market mainly.

Before I went to this appointment I had to wash my hair, which was a tangled mess. Then, because it was a very cold morning, Jack insisted I dry it properly before we went out. So by the time we'd made ourselves a cup of coffee and walked down over the railway footbridge to the Unemployment offices it was a good hour and a half later, around ten o'clock. We went in and saw the lady on reception.

'Mr Adams?' she said. 'We've got no Mr Adams.'

'You must have,' said Jack. Then he turned to me, shaking his head slowly. 'There's something definitely not right here. Are you sure it wasn't the DSS?'

The lady went away to make a phone call to the DSS to see if there was anyone there called Mr Adams. 'No,' she said, coming back, 'they've got no record of a Mr Adams either. But it mightn't be a bad idea if you went over there just to check.'

So we walked round the corner to the high street, where the DSS was. No, they had no Mr Adams either. Jack was seriously worried now.

'Come on,' I said to him, 'we'll go back to the B and B and wait there and see if he phones again.'

On the long road back out of town we ran into this

elderly lady who had the room above us at the B and B. She was just going down to the market to do some shopping. 'Oh,' she said, 'there was another phone call for you just now. Someone rang up and said, "Have they left yet?"'

We just looked at each other.

'Who was it?' asked Jack.

'It was a man.'

'What did he sound like?'

She was looking at me. 'He sounded a bit like her.'

Jack had gone drip-white, because we knew then that something was definitely up.

'Come on,' he said. He grabbed my hand and pulled me quickly over the road and into this café. It might seem strange that we didn't fully click what had happened straight away, but it was almost as if we were in a daze.

'Right,' Jack said, 'let's get to a phone box, let's call back the DSS, let's see what the hell's going on.' It was lucky we did, because when Jack got through to the same DSS woman she said, 'Thank God you rang! Just two minutes after you left three Indian men came in claiming to be her brothers. Looking for you.'

JACK:

I just went, 'Fucking hell!' I looked at Zena and I said, 'Right, that's it! They've found us! They're in the fucking town!' Instantly I knew what had happened. The social security information had leaked. Some Asian friend of theirs within the DSS had given them our whereabouts. Why else would they have gone straight to the DSS?

She grabbed my arm. 'There's a police station round the corner,' she shouted. 'Come on!'

We came out of that phone box like Linford Christie, sprinted across the road, round the back of the marketplace and threw ourselves into this sub-police station that Zena, luckily, had spotted the day before.

It was a tiny place, just a couple of rooms, with two

police officers running it, a man and a woman. They were an odd pair, both unusually tall, even for the Old Bill. PC Andrew was also exceptionally well built – definitely the kind of copper you'd hope wouldn't be first out of the panda to chase you if you were caught on a mission. WPC Monica was thin, but with her sharp cheekbones and short-cropped hair pretty tough-looking too. For the first time in my life I was relieved to be inside a police station.

We sat down with them in their little office and told them the complete story. There was a traffic warden hanging around in the background, ears flapping, but we couldn't be worrying about that. At least he was English. The two PCs listened patiently and sympathetically.

In a situation like that the natural course of action for the police is to put your name through the computer and see what they've got on you. So I was expecting, when we'd finished, to be nicked.

'I might as well tell you now,' I said. 'One – I've got a record. And two – there's a warrant out for my arrest for an unpaid fine.'

PC Andrew didn't seem too fazed by this. 'Right,' he replied, 'we'll get that sorted out, then.'

So we sat waiting. We could see him over at his desk, talking on the phone, obviously checking us out with the force in our home city. 'Ah, right,' he was saying, 'yes, yes.' But he wasn't looking at me, he was looking over at Zena. What the hell's going on here? I was thinking. He put the phone down and came over.

'So is that all right?' I asked.

'You're all right, mate,' he replied. 'Your fine's been blown out.' (I hadn't realized this, but after a certain period of time an unpaid fine is written off.) 'But,' he went on, 'your lass is wanted for a nine-thousand-pound theft charge.'

'You *what*?' I said.

'There's been a theft charge lodged against her by her family.'

'You've got to be joking,' I said. I looked over at Zena. She was visibly shaking.

'It's not true,' she said.

PC Andrew was sympathetic. 'What we're going to have to do,' he said, 'is take you down to the main nick in Grimsby and get this sorted out, OK?'

So the pair of them locked up the sub-station and drove us through Grimsby to the main police station on the other side of town. Despite this shock about the theft charge, I was still keeping a lookout for Zena's brothers. In particular Kasim's distinctive car, with its JAT 1 numberplate.

When the police searched us they found, of course, the two knives we'd been given by Vince and Gary, hooked in their leather sheaths to the backs of our trousers. We were cautioned for possessing offensive weapons and then they took Zena off to a cell and me to this room that was no bigger than a broom cupboard. 'You stay there while we sort this out,' said the duty sergeant, turning the key on me. After a while PC Andrew appeared. He gave me the kind of level-eyed look that coppers do if they know you've got form. 'So,' he said, 'What's the crack?'

'It's not true,' I told him. 'Our lass isn't the type to steal nine thousand pounds from her own family, whatever they've threatened.'

'And you,' he went on, 'with your record?'

'No disrespect to your town,' I replied, 'but if we had nine grand on us d'you really think we'd come to Grimsby? It'd be the last place on God's earth we'd come.'

PC Andrew took the point. He gave me a thin smile.

'Why don't you go back to our B and B,' I went on, 'and check it out? Search our room, search our bags, see for yourself, we haven't got a penny. I mean, do we look like we've got nine thousand?'

'I get the feeling,' PC Andrew replied, 'that what you're telling me is the truth. But we still have to go through the official procedures, I'm afraid. There's officers coming down from your local force to pick up your lass and question her.'

'They'll be taking us both back?'

'No, they're just coming for her. They'll probably let you go.'

'But them arseholes are still in town. Anyway, she can't go back on her own. I've got to be with her.'

'Look,' he said, 'all I know is there's officers coming down and any decisions that get made about who goes won't be made by me.'

'Well, can I see our lass now?'

'I'll see what we can sort out.'

ZENA:
After they'd cautioned us for the knives, these two WPCs took me through to this room and made me empty out my handbag and pockets on to a table. Why are they doing this? I thought. That's a bit disgusting of them, going through all my personal stuff. I didn't understand till later that that was what happened to everybody.

Then this one strongly built blonde woman led me off down a little corridor with the metal cell doors on either side. We got to one with an open door and I was just about to go in when she said, 'You'll have to take off your boots, coat and belt.'

'What am I going to put on my feet?' I protested. 'It's freezing – there's a stone floor in there.'

'I'm sorry. You'll have to leave them out here with your belt.'

So I pulled out my belt, kicked off my boots and crept in in my socks. I'd never seen the inside of a cell in my entire life. There was just a thin mattress on a hard wooden bench to sit on. The walls were covered with scrawled writing: rude words, rude suggestions, I love so-and-so, I miss so-and-so, big hearts. In the corner was a toilet. There was a button above it you had to press if you wanted them to flush it. It stank.

I had my Aran sweater with me, so after I'd used this disgusting toilet I rolled it up to use as a pillow and lay down on the mattress. It was so filthy I didn't want my face touching it. Then I just started to sob.

I couldn't believe that my own family had done this to me. Reduced one of their own flesh and blood to this. If they could see me now, I thought ... Then, as the time passed, I grew more and more angry. You're all right, I was thinking. You're all sitting in a warm house with food and all the luxuries you want. And here I am, locked in this stinking little cell. *How could you do this to me?*

Eventually the door opened and the blonde policewoman appeared again. 'D'you want a solicitor?' she asked.

'Can I see Jack?'

'No, that's not possible at the moment. But you do have the right to see a solicitor. Is there anyone in particular you'd like us to contact?'

The only solicitor I could think of in the world, let alone Grimsby, was the woman we'd seen the week before, Caroline Brown. So I asked them to phone that firm for me. A little while later the policewoman came back. 'D'you want a cup of tea?' she asked. 'Or something to eat?'

'Yeah, please, thank you.'

She brought me a beaker of machine tea and a plastic-looking cheese sandwich. But though I was hungry I just couldn't force it down at all. I was so scared about what was going to happen. They'd take me back home. They'd hand me back to my family. And then what would happen? I'd be sent straight to Pakistan on the plane. They'd break my legs so I'd never walk again, never get away again. They'd break my fingers so I could never write, never let Jack know where I was, never get out of there.

I'd had a cousin, Salmia, who'd been sent home to Pakistan and forced into a marriage. She'd thought, like us, she was going on a holiday, but it was for a wedding. The way her husband's family treated her was unbelievable. If she did something wrong – if the cooking didn't taste right, if the water pails weren't attached to the donkey correctly, whatever – they'd punish her for it. The women as well as the men. They used to starve her and hit her and strip her naked and sit her in the corner of her hut on a cold floor. She tried to write home but her mail was stopped. Eventually she managed to get one letter through to her brother. He blew all his savings to fly out and rescue her.

I lay there thinking of Salmia, wondering how much worse they'd treat me, who'd broken all the rules. Once they'd sent me back they'd go looking for Jack and God only knew what they'd do to him. I knew what families had done to other Asian men who'd messed around with their women; what they would do with an Englishman didn't bear thinking about.

The door clanked open again and the policewoman was back. 'Your solicitor's here,' she said. But it wasn't Caroline Brown, it was a colleague of hers, a dowdy-looking older man in a rumpled grey suit and glasses. I sat up and the policewoman gave me a handkerchief to dry my eyes.

This solicitor sat on one end of the mattress and I explained that this was a false allegation; there was no way I'd taken the money; did I look as if I had nine thousand pounds? My family were just using this to get me back home. If they were going to have to take me back up there, wouldn't it be possible for him to organize for Jack to come too? He listened, and nodded along. 'I'm very sorry,' he said at the end, 'but there's nothing much I can do for you.'

'What d'you mean?'

'This is out of our county, I'm afraid, so I can't help. All I can do is say "Good luck."' And with that he got up, shook my hand and walked out of the cell.

I was gobsmacked. Because I really had thought there would be some official way he could help me.

JACK:

Five minutes after he'd questioned me PC Andrew returned and led me down to one of those partitioned cells with a perspex grille in the middle. They let me in one side and brought Zena in on the other. She was in a right state. But I could see she was trying to keep her head and not break down completely.

The hole in the grille was so narrow I couldn't even hold her hand. 'Don't worry,' I told her, 'you're going to be safe, I'm going to make sure they take us both up there together, we're going to be together in a minute. The officers'll come from home, then we'll get back there and we'll explain everything and we'll be able to get some sort of proper help.'

We were best off where we were, I reassured her; at least we were safe. Zena just nodded blankly. It wasn't the old confident Zena at all.

We hadn't been together five minutes when PC Andrew came back in. 'Right,' he said. 'That's enough now.'

'But we only just—'

'Come on,' he said. I got to my feet and pushed my hand up against the grille. 'If the worst comes to the worst, love,' I said, 'and they don't let me up there, go to Ryan's. I'll make my way there.'

'If you can't get back to the B and B,' she called after me, 'go back to the bar and find those lads, Vince and Gary. They'll help you.'

Then the door was clanged shut and I was back up the stairs into the broom cupboard. This new copper came in, an altogether higher-ranking officer. He was older, with steel-grey hair and seriously chunky arms under his rolled-up sleeves.

'The officers from your home force are here,' he said briskly. 'They're taking your lass back home but they don't want to bother with you.'

'But I can't stop in Grimsby,' I protested. 'I can't go

back to the B and B. Her brothers'll more than likely be there waiting for me.'

There's nothing we can do about that,' he said.

'Well, can I stop here?'

'No. We've got no proof that there's any real harm likely to come to you.'

I couldn't believe what he was saying. He'd heard our full story. Why didn't he believe me?

'I've cautioned you now,' he continued, as he took me upstairs, 'and you'll have to leave.' He escorted me to the front door of the nick.

On the steps I shouted back at him. 'Which way are you taking her out?'

'They'll be coming out this way,' he told me.

So I waited by the corner of this little private access road, up against the wall in the shadows. At least I'll be able to see Zena, I thought. 'Thumbs up!' I planned to shout, as she was taken away. 'It'll all be all right, love.'

An hour later it was dark and there was still no sign of her. So I went back inside to see what was going on. 'Oh,' said the officer on the front desk, 'they've taken her out the back way. They left about an hour ago.'

The bastard had lied to me. Zena had been taken home. Obviously I had no idea what would happen when she got back to our county. But whatever the Old Bill decided, it was totally out of my control. I just had to pray that they wouldn't hand her back over. This may sound odd coming from someone who's had more than a few brushes with the law, but I reckoned that if anyone was going to understand how serious a position she was in it'd be the coppers back home. And I had this strong gut feeling that they wouldn't hand her back to her family. She was twenty-one, an adult, she had rights that the police were obliged to respect. I had to assume it was going to be OK. They'd hold her until I could get back up there.

Meantime I had to look out for myself. I didn't have a

penny on me and I knew for certain that her brothers were
in town.

ZENA:
When Jack had been taken away the blonde WPC had
come in again and told me to get ready. I was led up to a
big room full of desks and filing cabinets and introduced
to the two officers who'd come to take me home – a thickset
man and a skinny woman with her hair in a ponytail.

'Can't I bring my fiancé with me?' I pleaded. 'My
brothers are here in Grimsby with a professional hitman.
They're going to kill him if they catch up with him.'

That wasn't their problem, they said. It was only me
they were authorized to take; the theft charges were against
me. I was frantic. They didn't seem to understand the
seriousness of the situation; didn't even seem to believe
me, that Jack's life was in danger. 'He's got to come back
with me,' I was crying.

'Sorry, love,' they said. 'You're on your own.' And they
signed this form, took me outside and bundled me into the
back of a police car and drove off.

Now, as we sped through the darkness, the two officers
silent in the front, in addition to being worried sick about
Jack, left alone on the streets of Grimsby, I was in a total
panic about what was going to happen when I got home.
After a while we pulled into a garage to get some petrol.
'I hope you don't mind me asking,' I said to the WPC
when the male officer had got out, 'but my family's not
going to be at the police station, are they?'

'Nobody's going to be there except you.'

'What happens if they find out you've brought me back?'

'They're not going to find out,' she replied. For half an
hour or so I felt a wave of relief pass over me; but as we
came off the motorway into our city I could see the football
ground and the park and the rooftops of our area, and I
couldn't stop myself, I was really scared that they'd just

been reassuring me, telling me lies to keep me quiet, that Dad and Kasim would be waiting for me at the station and that would be it. I'd never see Jack again and who knew what punishment I would have to endure for my disobedience.

JACK:

I had nowhere to stay in Grimsby except the B and B, so I thought I'd better go back there. At least to have a look, see what was happening. If all was clear I was going to try and nip a few quid off the landlord, grab the luggage and clear off. The one thing I knew was that I didn't want to hang around in Grimsby.

So I headed off across town, keeping well off the main road, down backstreets, footpaths and, once or twice, clambering through people's back gardens. I was shitting myself. Whatever else, I thought as I went, at least Zena's OK. So long as she's in custody, she's safe. I can look after myself.

When I got back to the B and B I slunk up behind the wall over the road and had a good look. *The lights were on in our room!* And over the road were three cars in a place I'd never seen cars parked before. Looking back on it now there was no reason why those cars should have been anything to do with the brothers, but my head was in such a state, having seen our lights on, that I immediately thought, That's them.

I turned on my heel and ran back into town. What I'd do, I decided, was go to the bar where we'd met Vince and Gary, the lads who'd given us the knives. It had been the last thing Zena had said to me: If the worst comes to the worst, go back to that hotel.

I was in luck. The lads were there, up at the bar with a pint each in front of them. Thank God, I thought. At least there's somebody I can talk to. 'The shit's really hit the fan,' I told them. 'They've nicked our lass and taken her

103

home. They're saying she's taken nine grand . . .' My words were tumbling out any old how and at the end of the story I just came out with, 'The thing is, I need a bed for the night. Can you do anything?'

Vince paused for a second or two and looked over at Gary. Then, 'Yeah, mate,' he said, 'you'll be sound. We'll finish up here and then we'll go back to our lass's.' Jesus, I was grateful for that. Being the local amateur middleweight boxing champion, Vince had muscles and he clearly knew how to use them. Gary looked as if he could take care of himself, too. I was starting to feel, if not safe, at least that I had some friends to look after me.

When I'd got a pint down me and calmed down a bit I nipped into the phone booth at the end of the bar and put through a reversed-charge call to Ryan at home. I told him about the brothers turning up in Grimsby.

'You're not going to believe this,' I said, 'but they've got her on a nine-thousand-pound theft charge . . .'

'You've got to be joking . . .'

'No. They've taken her back. Looks like I might have to hitch up in the morning.'

'For fuck's sake, be careful, Jack. I haven't got a motor I can get my hands on right now or I'd be down to pick you up.'

'I'm all right. But look, I've told her if the Old Bill chuck her out to go up to yours. Is that OK?'

' 'Course it is. And if you do come up, make sure you get straight over here too. We'll look after you.'

When I put the phone down I headed back to the bar feeling a whole lot better. They were marvellous, Vince and Gary. I hadn't a penny on me but they stood me drinks all evening. By closing time Vince was in a pretty confident mood, waxing lyrical about his ability to see off any attack from the brothers.

'The thing is,' I said, as we left the hotel, 'I think we should stick to the backstreets. I don't want to risk the main road. They might still be here.'

'Oh no,' said Vince. 'You'll be all right with me, mate.'

I'd had a few to drink but not as many as him. Real fear, in any case, is a sobering thing. I knew for a fact that if three or four cars were to pull up beside us he'd most likely collapse on the pavement and I'd have to do a runner and leave him.

It was a good half-hour through the backstreets to his house. What he'd neglected to tell me until now was that he'd recently had a huge row with his wife. They'd only just got back together again and here he was turning up with this complete stranger who, if not totally cooked, had had a few – who he'd invited to spend the night. I was apprehensive, to say the least. But when we got there she seemed calm enough. Maybe he did this sort of thing all the time.

'Vince,' I said, as soon as we'd got in, 'I'm going to have to use your phone.'

He was a great fellow, didn't have a qualm about this. 'Of course, mate, yeah, use it,' he said. So I phoned the central police station back home and luckily got straight through to the officer who had booked Zena in. I told him my name and was just starting on, 'I believe you've got my fiancée up there . . .' when he replied, 'Thank *God* we know where you are.'

ZENA:

When we got to the county police station back home the male officer got in front of me and the WPC got behind me and they shuffled me up the steps like that and through the front double doors.

It was after eleven at night and the reception area was empty except for this clutch of officers by the front desk. The tall, sandy-haired one who was in charge had a look on his face that made me feel he was going to understand whatever it was I told him. There's going to be no messing around with this one, was my immediate thought.

'I haven't done it,' I blurted out. 'I haven't taken anything.'

'Come on, love,' he said, and he hurried me into a side room to take my details. 'Don't worry,' he went on, 'you're going to be all right here. We've taken all the Asian officers off the beat for the night. We're not going to put you in a cell. We're going to take you down to an interview room and someone'll come and talk to you there. Now, do you want a solicitor present?'

I had a name that Jack had given me. While they were trying to make contact with this man I explained what had happened in Grimsby; how they'd refused to bring Jack up with me and discharged him when we knew my brothers were still down there looking for us.

'*What* have they done?' said this officer.

'Yeah. They've thrown him out.'

'Right,' he went, and he immediately picked up the phone in front of me and got through to Grimsby. 'This ain't a game they're playing here!' I heard him shout down the line. 'What they're telling you is real.'

He obviously had a good idea of how seriously Asian communities view these things, because he was really giving this officer a piece of his mind. When he'd put the phone down he shook his head slowly from side to side. 'You don't need to say any more,' he told me. 'We have training courses for this kind of thing up here.'

At *last*, I thought, watching him, somebody is taking us seriously, somebody understands that this isn't all a joke. They took me down to this interview room and I was introduced to a PC Hutchinson. He was a really nice man as well, though about as different physically from his colleague as you could get, very slim and wiry. He had a stutter, too.

'The tape's broken, I'm afraid,' he said, 'so we can't record you. I'll have to take your statement by hand.'

I repeated what Jack had told me to say. 'D'you really think,' I said, 'that if we had nine thousand pounds on us we'd have settled in Grimsby? My fiancé has told them down there that we wouldn't settle in Grimsby . . .'

'Right, that's fine, calm down,' said PC Hutchinson. 'Now I'm going to formally read you the charge, OK? Your family say that you've taken restaurant earnings and a whole lot of gold jewellery from home . . .'

'I haven't taken anything. The only gold I had was two bangles that were my personal possessions which we pawned in Sheffield for four hundred pounds.'

'It's OK, calm down,' he repeated. 'We believe you.' And he took down my statement denying the charges.

Then he asked if I wanted to press charges against my own family. If I did, it would have to be done in a court of law here in our home city. So I refused. I didn't want to face my family across a courtroom, furious though I was with them all.

After he'd written up my statement PC Hutchinson took me back up to the charge desk where they had the solicitor waiting on the phone for me. He had spoken to the officers and I was free to go now, he said.

If I wanted anywhere to stay there was an Asian Women's Refuge where I could spend the night. But I wasn't having any of that. I'd heard about this Asian Women's Refuge before. It was notorious for handing young women and girls back to their families in return for large cash payments.

'I don't trust them there,' I said to the blond senior officer. 'If I'm not staying here in the station I either want to go to my fiancé's brother or back to Grimsby.' (Jack had phoned in the meantime and spoken to the desk sergeant, so we knew where he was.)

'Well, I wouldn't go up to his brother's if I were you,' said this officer. 'The chances are they're going to have that place staked out. I think what we'd better do is get a car to take you back down to Grimsby.'

On the front steps he said goodbye. 'After this,' he went on, 'we really don't want to know where you're going. If your family somehow finds out that you've been here we don't want to have anything to give them.'

Kindly, stuttering PC Hutchinson was there too. 'If you do ever want to get in touch with us,' he said, 'or you want to ring and find out if anything has been going on with the family, feel free to pick up the phone.'

JACK:
'Thank *God* we know where you are,' said this copper down the phone.

'You're aware of our situation?'

'We've got your lass in the interview room right now. She's told us your story. Are you all right?'

This was a bit of a different attitude. 'I'm all right,' I said, 'but what's happening with Zena?'

She was fine, he said. They didn't believe the theft-charge story. 'We're just going to take her statement and then we'll bring her back down to you.'

'I'm not sure you can bring her to this place I'm staying. It's a bit tricky—'

Vince was standing just near me shaking his head. 'No, mate,' he interrupted. 'Can't afford to have the Old Bill outside the door at this time of night, the wife's going to go berserk—'

'No, no,' came the voice of this officer from home. 'We wouldn't bring her to a private address in any case. It's too risky, with the situation you're both in. We'll take her to the main station.'

'What time d'you reckon you're going to get down here?'

'Around three in the morning.'

'All right,' I said. 'Tell her to wait there whatever happens. I'll make my way over and pick her up.'

I explained the situation to Vince. I couldn't leave Zena in the nick for the night. She'd had a traumatic enough time for one day without being locked back in a cell. Would it be OK, I asked, if I went and got her and brought her back to his place?

'Yeah, no problem,' he said. He'd had a coffee and sobered up a bit by now. His wife had gone to bed. 'How're you going to get back over there?' he asked.

'I don't know. I haven't got a penny.'

'Nor me,' he laughed. 'Not after that evening.' He dropped his voice. 'I can't nip the wife, obviously.'

'Fair enough.'

'I'll take a walk over with you. If they see you on your own . . .' He shrugged and made a face. 'They might think different if there's a couple of us.'

So we left his house and made our way back through town to the police station, keeping our eyes skinned for any trouble. I was still very much on edge. But it was two in the morning and the place was dead. If Kasim and the others were still in town they weren't cruising round looking for us.

For one bit of the walk we had to come off the backstreets on to the big main road. Just as we turned the corner a police car suddenly shot past us, blue light flashing. There was Zena, huddled in the back. I only caught a glimpse in silhouette but it was definitely her.

'Eh, Vince,' I said. 'That's our lass just passed us.'

He laughed. 'Shit. They could have stopped.'

Eventually we got over there and after half an hour or so Zena came out into reception. She looked relieved, but utterly drained. 'Oh, Jack,' she cried and threw herself into my arms.

We had to make our own way back to Vince's house. The Grimsby force didn't offer us any protection, not even a lift over there. They were going to make some arrangements for us the next day, they said. We would have to report back in the morning. Despite the dressing down Zena had heard them getting from the officer at home, they still didn't seem to be taking our situation that seriously.

In the morning PCs Andrew and Monica were waiting for us at the Grimsby nick. They drove us in a van straight to the Unemployment offices.

There was no hanging around in the crowded waiting room this time. We were led straight through to the back, to this room that was clearly the DSS nerve-centre, full of computer screens and, in the middle, the machine that prints out the giros.

Immediately we were given the cheque we'd been waiting for for ten days. 'It's amazing,' I murmured to Zena, 'what a couple of coppers in uniform can do to speed up your giro.'

I thought we might as well make the most of this special treatment we were getting. So I asked to see the manager, who was instantly made available.

'It's obvious to me,' I said, when we were alone in his office, 'that there's only one place the information about us being in Grimsby could have come from, and that's here. Nobody else knew our names and addresses. But as soon as we've gone on computer, here, they've surfaced and found us.'

'I've got to agree with you,' he replied. 'It does look that way.'

He apologized to me personally for the lapse in security and said he'd make sure it didn't happen again, by putting us on what is known as the National Sensitive register. VIPs like the Home Secretary were on it, he told me. It basically meant that nobody in any other office could tap into the system with your details and find out where you were claiming.

This sounded great. The only problem was that it took five to six weeks for the new status to go nationwide. 'So if you can help it,' he said, 'don't make another claim for six weeks.'

'Fair enough.'

'And in the meantime I promise you there'll be a full investigation.'

Zena and I were happy enough with that. We'd got our payment at last – that was the main thing.

'Right,' said PC Andrew, 'we'll take you back to your bed and breakfast.' He was as wary as we were by this time. That same traffic warden who had been in the sub-station when we'd told the police our story the day before had actually been stopped by Zena's brothers and asked for directions. PC Andrew had known it was them because the warden had noticed the distinctive numberplate, JAT 1.

'It wouldn't surprise me,' PC Andrew said now, 'if they were in there waiting for you. They might even have to come to some arrangement with the landlord.'

Zena's original reservations about the landlord were justified. He was well known to the police, apparently.

PC Andrew led the way. Then WPC Monica. Then me. Then Zena at the rear. It was mid-morning and there didn't seem to be a soul in the place. We got our key from its hook. Then PC Andrew crept along the corridor, unlocked the door and, finger to his lips, suddenly burst in. The room was empty. Our stuff was just as we'd left it.

'Right,' he said, 'we need to get out of here as quickly as possible. Gather up what you need and we'll be off.'

So we jammed as much as we could into our bags and scarpered. The two officers took us to the post office to cash our giro. Then we returned to the nick for an interview with the same grey-haired bastard who'd shown me the door before. He was altogether gentler with us this time.

'The best thing we can do for you at the moment,' he told us, 'is to get you moved from here. Because obviously your family know where you are now.'

The plan was to shift us over the county line to Lincoln. Contact had been made with the force there and we'd be looked after and sorted out with somewhere safe to stay. PCs Monica and Andrew would take us down there in an unmarked car.

This all seemed reasonable enough to us. In the shocked

and exhausted state of mind we were in we were grateful just to be looked after. As we sped south that afternoon I just felt relieved that each minute was taking us a mile further from Grimsby.

9

JACK:
PC Andrew and WPC Monica said their goodbyes and
wished us luck and left us there in West Gate, which is the
main nick in Lincoln. It had been arranged, they'd told us,
that Zena was going to be met by a representative from a
women's refuge and taken there for the night while I found
myself a B and B. I wasn't too delighted with this idea –
especially with our being separated – but there wasn't a
lot I could do. For the time being, at least, we were in their
hands.

We sat waiting together on a bench in the draughty
front reception area. About half an hour after the Grimsby
officers had left, this woman arrived from the refuge. She
wore baggy corduroy trousers, little round glasses, and had
unkempt dark hair. No disrespect to feminists, but she
really was the cliché. I don't think she'd even been told
that I was going to be there. She went straight up to Zena.
'Don't worry, love,' she was saying, 'we'll get you somewhere safe tonight.' When I suddenly stood up she looked
at me as if to say, 'Who the hell's this?'

I was trying to be friendly. 'Well, look,' I said as she led
Zena off, 'I'll walk up there with you.'

'Oh no,' she replied, 'I'm sorry, I can't allow you to
come anywhere near the hostel. I can't even tell you where
it is.'

I thought, We've just been through all this drama
together and now you're telling me I can't even see where
Zena's staying. What d'you think I'm going to do? Grass
up all the other women that are in there? I really don't

give a shit about them, it's our lass I'm concerned about.

But in the circumstances I thought it was best if I just accepted the fact that she wanted to take Zena up there alone. So we made an arrangement that as soon as I'd found myself a B and B I'd phone back the police station so Zena would know where I was. Then I kissed her good-bye, and off they went.

I walked out of the nick, down the steps, and into the middle of Lincoln. Which was a place I'd never been before in my life. Right, I said to myself, the first thing I'm going to do is get myself a pint. And I walked straight off the street into this pub that was probably the only gay bar in Lincoln. All these men were sitting up at the bar with these gaudy little waistcoats on. I don't give a shit, I thought, as I joined them. I've had enough. I'm having a beer and that's that.

ZENA:
I'd been left with this lady in the corduroy trousers. She was terribly pale and skinny with long scraggly hair. Mine was all tangled because my hairbrush had been stolen from Grimsby station and we hadn't been able to afford a new one, but hers seemed to be unwashed and unbrushed deliberately.

I don't know whether she'd had a very tough life or what, but she looked totally dead behind the eyes. She was pushing a buggy with a baby in it, and there was a young girl with her who couldn't have been more than about eight or nine. She was frail-looking, this child, but the woman made her carry one of my bags. 'It's all right,' I said, 'it's a rucksack, I can throw it over my shoulder.' But no, she was insistent that this poor kid carry the bag. 'She's fit,' she said. And believe it or not – I didn't think she'd make it – that little scrap of a girl hauled my heavy rucksack right up that steep hill.

The women's refuge was a tall old terraced house, all

sectioned off into individual bedrooms with a communal area downstairs. The woman took me in and up the stairs to a little attic room at the top. 'I'll leave you here to settle yourself in,' she said. 'Come down when you're ready and we'll make you a bite to eat.'

I chucked my bags on the bed and walked over to the window. You could see right down over Lincoln, miles and miles of streetlamps and rooftops and dark trees. I was wondering where Jack had got to out there. Then I found myself thinking: I can't stay here. It just didn't feel right.

I went downstairs to the kitchen-laundry area and sat at one end of this big old pine table where a few of the other women were sitting chatting and reading magazines and newspapers. One of them, quite a young woman, jumped up when I came in and offered to fry me up some eggs and chips. Another, a big, red-haired lady, said, 'So where d'you come from? With that accent it sounds like Yorkshire.'

I said nothing.

'I come from Yorkshire,' she went on, and as soon as she said that I thought, No, I'm not stopping here. I was still in a panic after what had happened in Grimsby. I didn't want there to be even the slightest risk of anyone from home finding out where we'd moved on to. And this woman asking these questions was freaking me out totally.

I turned to one of the other girls. 'Have you got a warden or somebody that's on in the evening?' I asked. But they didn't even have a warden, and I couldn't find the lady who'd brought me here anywhere, so I just ran back upstairs and picked up all my bags and left. I didn't feel safe there at all. I wanted to be with Jack.

It was pitch-dark outside. There was no streetlighting on that hill. I just scurried down it with my bags. It was so steep I thought I'd tumble down it. I ran into the police station and reported at the desk. 'Has Jack Briggs rung?' I asked. No, the sergeant said, there'd been no call from a Jack Briggs.

'I'm expecting him to ring. When he calls could you tell him his wife's here waiting for him and could he come down and collect her from the police station.'

'OK, love,' said the sergeant.

So I sat there waiting in this freezing, draughty reception area. There was a group of youths standing right by the front door waiting for one of their mates to come out. They were calling, 'Paki, Paki,' and other bits of racial abuse. Nobody stopped them so I just tried to ignore it; they were just foolish kids who'd had a couple to drink. But I was getting edgier and edgier in case they started causing real trouble. And what on earth had happened to Jack? Why hadn't he called back? If he didn't call where would I stay? I had no money and I couldn't go back to that refuge now. I just didn't feel safe there.

After about an hour I was getting desperate. I went back up to the desk to enquire again. As I was waiting, a new officer came out of a side door. 'Are you Zena Chadhaury?' he asked.

'Yeah.'

'Are you expecting a phone call?'

'I've been sat here waiting for one for the past hour.'

'I'm sorry, it's come through to the other switchboard.' Jack had left a message over half an hour before.

'Come through here, love.' He took me through to another room and sat me down at an interview desk. 'Right,' he said, 'give me a few details of your fiancé.'

'Well,' I began, 'he's about five foot ten, he's got tattoos on his hands, he's losing his hair . . .'

'That's fine,' said this officer, as if he was checking the details of a lost suitcase. 'We'll take you down there.'

JACK:
I'd meanwhile had this very bad gut feeling about that women's refuge. I just knew there was something wrong. So as soon as I'd finished my pint and found myself a bed

116

and breakfast I'd phoned the police station to see if she'd called. It took me a while to get through. No, the duty officer told me when I finally managed to get an answer, they hadn't heard from her.

Now I got this call saying could I wait in the street outside the bed and breakfast. Soon enough a panda car drew up with Zena and her luggage in the back. A copper jumped out and walked straight up to me. 'Let's have a look at your hands,' he said, grabbing them.

'What the . . .' I began.

'Oh yes, you're him all right,' he said. One hand was inscribed with my name, the other with the name of a girl I'd been involved with a long time before. (Very young, very drunk and very foolish I'd been when I'd had those done.) After that little show of respect they told us to report back to the nick in the morning.

So, the next day, after the usual safari with Zena's bags, we were shown eventually into a private interview room. We'd only been waiting there about ten minutes when the door flew open and in walked PC Alan Jones. He was a tall man, six-two, maybe six-three, slim, with a neatly clipped head of fawnish hair. The vibes were immediately good. We've been lucky enough, I thought, to stumble upon a decent copper.

'Right,' he said, as if this was the first time we'd ever been inside a police station. 'Could you give us a little background?' At Grimsby we'd been given the strong impression that we were being sent to Lincoln as part of a coherent plan. Now it was clear that not only had there been no cross-county relaying of information, PC Jones knew nothing of our situation at all. We had to take him through the whole saga right from the beginning.

'OK,' he said, when we'd finished. 'I'm going to have to have a word with someone else about this.' (Much later, Alan told me that when he'd gone and relayed our story to his superior officer that morning the reaction had been, 'Ah, they're throwing you a line.' 'Come and look at them,' had been Alan's response. 'When you see them you'll believe it.' Thinking about it since, I've often thought: God only knows what would have happened to us if we'd had a less sympathetic officer than PC Jones. Or if he hadn't gone the extra mile to persuade his superior to see us.)

Now this senior officer came in and we went through our tale yet again. When he heard it directly from us he seemed quite genuinely horrified.

'Right,' he said, 'the first thing we're going to have to do is make sure this job's done properly. First off, we're going to have to get you somewhere safe to stay until we can get you sorted out. If it's OK with you,' he went on, 'I'm going to get someone from Victim Support down here to have a word with you.'

'That's fine,' I said, looking over at Zena with quiet amazement. The more professionals, I reckoned, we could get to hear about our situation, the more seriously we were going to be taken, the more help we were going to get.

So PC Jones and this senior officer led us up through the station, past the bar area, and left us in a little room at the back. And an hour or so later Jones returned with a woman called Margaret Jackson. As Zena said, she looked exactly like a younger version of the Queen, with a Scottish accent. The long tweed skirt and expensive-looking satin waistcoat she was wearing could have been part of the royal wardrobe, too.

Once again we went through our story. Once again a head was shaken and we were told how appalling our situation was.

Alan Jones then quizzed us – Zena in particular – about the Muslim bounty hunter. He knew someone who was an expert in this field, he said, and he wanted to find out just how serious a threat this man really was. We carried on talking to Margaret Jackson, and after twenty minutes or so Jones came back, nodding quietly to himself. He looked from one to the other of us and said, 'This guy means business. I've had a word with someone who knows his methods and,' he paused and looked at the two of us, 'you wouldn't want to know the ins and outs of it.'

I took it for granted that we didn't want to know. But I felt quietly grateful that all our fears had not just been paranoia.

They had decided, they said, to transfer us to a safe house. This place was another B and B, but it was run by a woman who had once been an officer with the London Metropolitan Police. We were taken over there in a van and they told us our room would be fitted with a panic alarm. Then Jones and another officer made a sketch of the place, the access and the street outside. An armed response vehicle was going to be on full alert in the area. This is more like it, I thought.

Later that day Margaret Jackson came to see how we were settling in. Lincolnshire would provide protection in the short term, she explained. In the meantime we should sit down together and try to think of a place in the British Isles where we might feel safe for a more permanent move.

So that night we sat up in our room at this safe house working our way through all the cities and towns we knew. Everywhere I came up with Zena countered: 'No, I've got relatives there.' Coventry, Birmingham, Glasgow, Leicester, London, Reading, you name it. Eventually, as a joke, I suggested the Channel Islands – Jersey, or Guernsey. 'Don't tell me you've got relatives there.'

'No, I don't think I have.'

So the next day we suggested the Channel Islands. Margaret Jackson considered this proposal for a while. 'What about the Isle of Wight?' she asked. She had contacts who ran a women's refuge down there.

'That sounds great,' we told her. We had no clue what the place was like, but I immediately liked the sound of an island. One step further for anyone trying to follow us.

'I'll talk to them and see what we can do,' she said.

Things were less satisfactory with our new landlady, though, the ex-Met officer. The money we'd got from our crisis payment had run out (although this had been described as a safe house we were still paying full bed and breakfast rates). And she'd apparently been told we were only going to be there for one night.

'This fucken ain't on,' she was going, as we sat at the kitchen table on our second morning there. 'They want to make up their fucken minds what they *are* doing. How many fucken nights are you supposed to be here? I've got plans too, you know.'

It wasn't exactly the warmest welcome I'd ever had, and hardly what the words 'safe house' conjured up.

On the second evening PC Jones turned up out of uniform with a bin-bag full of old clothes. 'I've been rooting around in my place,' he said, 'and I've come up with some gear for you, Jack.' He'd brought the lot: boxer shorts, socks, T-shirts, jeans. I've met many coppers in my life – good, bad and ugly – but PC Jones was truly one of the best. This was completely his own initiative. He didn't have to do it, and it was highly appreciated, then and now.

As I sat there trying these things on he said, 'Have you thought of taking her abroad?'

'How could I afford that, Alan?'

'In your position,' he said, giving me the old level-eyed copper's look, 'I'd have robbed a bank and been out of the country by now.' He was, in all respects, an unusual policeman.

It was a question we were to be asked again, often. In answer I always made two points. One, I didn't see why I should have to take Zena abroad. England is my country and, on principle, I didn't see why I should be chased out of it because I happened to have fallen in love with the wrong woman – an Englishwoman born and bred, whatever her family's origins.

Two, I didn't *want* to go anywhere else. I may not be the most patriotic of people but I still think England is the best country in the world. Why? Freedom of speech, the NHS, the social services. That may sound laughable, considering everything we've been through, but I'm still sure that, given the circumstances, we've been better off here than anywhere else.

I don't want to live in a country where if you collapse on the streets the first thing they do is check to see if your credit card works. And the police here may not be perfect, but they're a whole lot better than in some countries where problem cases like us can just disappear without trace.

That is, I suppose, why I feel so strongly that the problem we are the living embodiment of needs to be sorted out. People died in wars to keep this a free country. And, in the sense that I cannot live in peace and quiet with the woman I love, it is no longer a free country.

The next day Margaret Jackson returned. The Isle of Wight was on! Funding had been found to get us down there and once we'd arrived, she told us, everything would be fine. Her friends at the refuge were completely sound and reliable people.

We were told now to think of new names for ourselves, as a first step towards the completely new identities we'd be creating for ourselves on the island. 'Michael Burnley' and 'Sonya Atkinson' were what we came up with. We decided we'd immediately start to use these names to each other, even in private, to get used to them. We practised our new signatures – Michael Burnley, Sonya Atkinson, Michael Burnley, Sonya Atkinson – over and over till we felt totally comfortable with them. Till we felt we would convince any official watching us sign a form.

Things were moving fast. Three days after we'd arrived in Lincoln, on the Friday morning, we left the safe house, said goodbye to PC Alan Jones (as we thought then for good), and Margaret Jackson drove us like the devil down to Peterborough.

Bless her – as she put us on the coach to London she was almost crying. 'All the best,' she said. 'You're going to be well looked after on the Isle of Wight, don't worry. They'll definitely get something sorted out for you down there. Keep in touch,' she added, as she hugged Zena and shook my hand.

And on that highly optimistic note we climbed on to the National Express coach and set off on the next leg of our unasked-for adventure.

ZENA:

I think it must have been something to do with the shock of yet another move, but as we sped south in the coach down the motorway I felt the same sharp pains in my lower stomach that I normally only get when my monthly cycle comes on. It can't be that, I thought; I'd only finished my last period in Grimsby, a week before. But as we came off the motorway I knew that I was bleeding again.

My mind was messed up, my body was messed up, I didn't know whether I was coming or going. Jack held my hand as the bus crawled through the traffic-blocked streets of London, which seemed as if they'd never end. Eventually we arrived at Victoria. I was scared to stand up, praying I hadn't got a stain on the cream-coloured trousers I was wearing.

Thankfully it was OK, but I had no towels. So I stood by our luggage in the drizzle as Jack ran into a chemist's over the road and fetched me some. Then I couldn't cope with the public toilet; so he got some pound coins so I could go into one of those private free-standing lavatories.

Jack had been through Victoria once before so he knew a little café round the corner where we could get a cheap meal. Once I'd cleaned myself up we went in there and dried off and had a coffee and a good scran. Then we were off again. Truly, I felt like a leaf blown in the wind. I didn't know what was happening to me.

10

JACK:

Margaret Jackson had given us this code word to greet the person who came to meet us at the hoverport. 'Hello, I notice the kippers are flying backwards today.' Something spyish like that – I can't remember the exact phrase. I'd assumed, this being a women's refuge group, that it would be a woman who would turn up to meet us.

There was a middle-aged lady standing outside the glass doors of the terminal, on her own, in a waxed green jacket and headscarf. Right, I thought, this must be the one. So I sidled up to her and said, 'Hello, I notice the kippers are flying backwards today,' or whatever, and she gave me this absolutely disgusted look and stalked off. Which I took to mean she was not the contact. Bloody good job I wasn't a spy in Berlin, I reckon.

There was no one else around so we crossed a little footbridge to the main car park. A battered green estate car pulled up and inside was a bearded Fisherman Sam type giving us very furtive looks. He must have been told, 'Look out for Morticia and Lurch, you'll spot 'em', because he came straight over and we went through this ridiculous greeting and then he helped us and our luggage into his car.

'What's new on the Mainland?' he asked. It was only a friendly remark but it immediately made me feel as if we'd come to another country. I'd had no idea that the Isle of Wight was so close to Portsmouth (I'd imagined it way out in the Channel) but even that narrow stretch of water had made us both feel a hundred times safer.

He was going to drive us over, he said, to one of the organizers of this women's refuge group, in Ventnor. She would put us up for a day or two while they got things sorted out. He only had a rough idea of our story but was pretty keyed up about what had happened to us. 'Don't worry,' he said, 'I've got plenty of friends with houses here. We can always move you about if we need to. And if the worst comes to the worst I've got mates with boats and we can ship you off somewhere else.' Great, I thought again, *at last* we're getting the understanding and support we need.

The road ran right along the coast, past tall cliffs dropping down to small sandy beaches, cottages with thatched roofs, tiny fields with old-fashioned hedgerows. Not only did it feel like another country, it looked like one too. After twenty minutes or so we arrived at Emma Hillier's cottage. It was a beautiful place, on a steep little lane above the sea. You could step out through the French doors on to this patio and just watch the waves rolling in.

Emma was young, still in her twenties I'd have guessed, quite serious-looking with her cropped hair and thick tortoiseshell glasses. 'You must be exhausted,' she said. 'I'll show you to your room. Just completely relax, right, and treat the place like home.'

She explained that over the next couple of days we were going to be introduced to the head of this women's organization, Brenda Steele, have a bit of a conference and work out where to go from here.

'By the way,' she added, 'my boyfriend's turning up tonight for the weekend. He's fine about your being here and I've not told him anything about your circumstances. He knows I'm involved with this movement, so if it's cool with you it's OK with us.'

We didn't care. It just felt good being treated like human beings again.

About seven o'clock this boyfriend appeared. Tom seemed very nice, very polite. 'You all right?' he asked, smiling as he put his head round the door. He didn't seem at all fazed about having us two scarecrows sitting there on his settee.

Before tea, the pair of them took us out for a drink in a little pub just down the hill. At the table next to us there was a bit of a fervent discussion going on about parking regulations. They were bringing in some new tariff on the island. 'And they *reverse* right into my *drive*,' this smartly dressed Hyacinth Bouquet woman was saying.

Emma leant towards us. 'As you can see,' she said, 'we get excited about the really big issues here on the island. Millions of people starving in the world and we're arguing about parking restrictions.'

We laughed. It was lovely to be out like that, just sitting there relaxing in a pub with conversations going on all around. The first time I'd been in such a normal situation since we'd left (had it really only been three weeks before?).

Zena says I drink too much and perhaps, given the chance, I do. But I've always associated pubs with the good times in life. At home, Sunday dinner always used to be what they'd call 'the best drink of the week'. Everybody would have saved a couple of quid and we used to have 'a cheekerin'. As long as you had enough for a pint you'd be in. From then on there'd be someone who'd get you a pint. There might be a bit of bar food, a juke box going, a bunch of guys sitting round a table, maybe a game of killer on the pool table. And if you won that you'd have twenty quid in your pocket and be set up for the whole evening.

After the weekend Brenda Steele turned up at the cottage. She was a big forthright woman with a mop of dark hair like a party wig. As Zena said, she was like Jo Brand but without the humour.

We were all sitting round in Emma's front room working out a plan and I was starting to get a bit edgy. I had the same feeling that I'd had with the refuge woman in Lincoln.

125

The discussions were going on fine but the whole thing seemed to be directed at Zena. I knew that they had been reluctant to take me on in the first place, and now, once again, I got that feeling of being extra baggage. Because I was a bloke. It was almost as if I wasn't in the room.

I resented that in a way because I thought of myself not necessarily as being the head honcho, but at least of being responsible for our safety and our movements. I just thought I should be included.

Back in Lincoln we had also been told that the police were going to be notified of our arrival, and that our first meeting would be between the women's refuge people and the police. But there were no coppers present. When I chipped in to ask about this, Brenda Steele's reaction was, 'No, we don't trust the police here. On the island.'

'But we're running for our lives,' I said. 'We need police protection. The police are essential to us.'

'The police down here have got very backward views. If it was one of their daughters they'd probably be doing the same.'

That's a bit of a strange attitude to take, I thought. But I decided to let it go. They had organized this house for us to stay in. They were being extremely helpful. Their plans seemed very well worked out. What they were going to do, they said, was take us off the island and get us married on the Mainland (as they called it) in our real names. Then they would bring us back and we could resume being Michael Burnley and Sonya Atkinson. That way we'd be properly married but nobody would be able to trace us through our wedding certificate. We'd be able to settle on the island. Our new contacts would hopefully be able to give us references. With luck we'd get jobs. Then we'd be able to leave charity and the State behind and get on, independently, with our new life together.

At last, we thought, *this is finally it*.

ZENA:

Emma was being so kind to us. We'd already been staying in her cottage for a week. Now she and her boyfriend Tom had to go to a wedding on the Mainland. Instead of chucking us out she handed us her house keys and told us we could have the place to ourselves. Then she gave us twenty pounds to buy food. 'If that's not enough,' she said, 'there's a jar full of coins in the kitchen, just help yourself.'

It was the first time since we'd run away that we'd actually been able to stop and feel secure. It was so lovely there. There was a fresh breeze off the sea, the sound of seagulls calling, of the waves crashing up the little beach below the house. Emma let us do exactly what we wanted: listen to music, watch videos. One day we took a walk down the hill into Ventnor, which was a sweet little toytown of a place.

'It's like stepping back in time,' Jack said, as we strolled around.

Perhaps because I was filled with a new mood of optimism we decided we'd phone home and see if anything had changed since we'd last spoken to them. Spring was coming; maybe they'd find it in their hearts, if not to forgive us at least to remove the death threat.

Jack phoned the restaurant for me and got Kasim. 'Just put my sister on,' he said abruptly. But when I picked up the receiver it wasn't Kasim – it was my father. Before I could say hello, it was, 'Where are you, Zena?'

'Dad, I can't say. But you've got to understand,' I rushed on, 'that we're going to get married whatever happens. All we want is that you should accept us—'

'Zena,' he interrupted, 'you can either come back home and we can rip up the marriage papers – that won't matter—'

'No, Dad,' I interrupted, 'I'm getting married to Jack and you've just got to accept—'

'You were meant to marry my nephew Bilal—'

'I'm not marrying Bilal, I'm marrying Jack, I don't love Bilal, what's Bilal got to do with me . . . ?'

'Bilal's who you were meant to marry, Zena. I went to Mecca to ask for a blessing on your marriage to Bilal—'

'Dad, I'm not coming home and I'm not marrying Bilal and that's final.'

'You died for me the day you left,' he said then. 'You can't hide from us for ever, Zena. When we catch up with you you're both dead.'

I'd never heard this awful, cold tone from him in my life before. Though he could be stern, he had always been loving. Now it was like talking to a stranger. Then he'd gone and I was in tears and Kasim was on. 'You tell Jack,' he repeated, 'that if you don't come home we're going to take one of his family out . . .' And he went off into a screaming rant again about how we were both going to end up in bin-bags and they would have stone-clad alibis and all that. I couldn't take any more of it so I just put the phone down. Then I slumped down on the sofa and just cried and cried.

'What did he say?' Jack was asking, as he put his arms around me, hugged me tight. I could hardly speak. 'Don't worry,' he went on, 'it's going to be OK, love. We'll get over this, it's going to be OK.'

But I couldn't see how it ever would be. I'd never imagined, in a million years, that my father could talk to me like that. It was just that deathly, impersonal tone.

I understood how angry he was. As he'd said, his pilgrimage to Mecca had been the greatest achievement of his life. If he'd prayed for Bilal and me then that was all bound up with that. But the way I saw it was that I wasn't meant for Bilal. I truly believe that the day I was born I was already written for Jack. That's how it felt to me, so strongly. So from a religious point of view I had done nothing wrong.

JACK:

What can you say at moments like that? I just put my arms around her and did my best to console her. 'Don't worry, we'll get over this, this is only a temporary setback, we're going to get through this . . .'

From my point of view, each time we moved further down this road with her family I couldn't believe what was happening. I understood that they came from a very different culture, that their religion meant so much to them. But now, for example, I couldn't stop thinking, What kind of a father says that to his own daughter? And all for what? Can't you take the hint that it's not going to happen? Can't you take this as a little bit of a sign that SHE IS NOT GOING TO MARRY YOUR NEPHEW?

I respect Zena's father's religion – he's entitled to his beliefs. Everyone is. But what I want to know is this: If they really believe in destiny, that everything's mapped out in advance, where do I fit in? Am I just a fly in the ointment? Zena and I love each other, we're *happy* together.

When Emma came back from her weekend on the Mainland we had another meeting with Brenda Steele. They told us that we were being moved out of the cottage and down to a B and B at Sandown. They didn't think it was a good idea for us to be at one address for too long, they said. For security's sake, it was best to keep moving. Fair enough, we thought.

So Emma drove us to Sandown and saw us into this little B and B on the seafront. She hugged us both like old friends, and gave us another five pounds to tide us over till we could sort out our welfare payments from the DSS the next day.

Everything seemed to be going so well for us on this magical island. Even the DSS was beautiful. The waiting room was comfortably furnished, there were flowers on the table, it was clean and carpeted, more like a proper office than anything to do with the dole. I felt like asking if I could sign up as a registered drunk, just to give the security guard something to do.

The officer in charge of our case, Susan Bates, had already been thoroughly briefed about our circumstances. Before we knew it we'd been given not only the complete payment for our bed and breakfast but an extra grant for me to buy some new clothes. We were allowed to claim in our new names – without fuss they issued us with temporary NI numbers. (For the long term we were asked to write letters to a National Insurance agent in Newcastle formally applying for us to become permanently National Sensitive.) Susan even gave us a payment book which meant that we didn't have to go into the office to sign on. All we had to do was sign a slip of paper, post it, and they'd send out the giro. We couldn't believe it.

ZENA:
The room we had at this new B and B in Sandown was tiny. The double bed took up so much space that you had to walk sideways to pass between the bed and the window; on the other side you could only open the wardrobe enough to squeeze a coat-hanger through. If the ceiling had been any lower we wouldn't have been able to stand up. Yet we were happy as anything to be there. It felt like a safe haven for us.

For the first time since we'd left home we could afford breakfast. It was the only hot meal we didn't share, and it was a treat to come down to each morning. We'd have coffee, toast, poached or scrambled eggs, and Jack would joke about how much he longed for bacon! He'd given up pork the previous autumn, as a sign, he said, of his love for me. Obviously pork is *haram* – forbidden – in our religion. It was a remark I'd made about being able to smell a pork pie on his breath that had sparked it off. 'All right, Zena,' he'd said, in that mock-courtly way he has when he's fooling around sometimes, 'for you I'll swear off the pork pie. Not to mention the bacon buttie.'

The amazing thing was – he'd stuck to it!

We didn't spend all the time cooped up in our room either. Every day we made sure we went out for a walk. On sunny mornings it was just about warm enough for us to sit out for an hour or two on the beach out of the wind.

Then the money came through for Jack's new clothes, so we went looking for bargains up and down Sandown High Street. He ended up with underwear, three T-shirts and two new pairs of jeans.

We were both sleeping at nights, too. At the same time, though not in the same place. We still stuck to the same arrangement we'd had all along: Jack took the quilt and slept on the floor, or across the end of the bed. I had the bedding, the sheets and the bed. Just because I'd run away from my family didn't mean I'd abandoned my religion, or the principles I'd learnt from that religion. It was very important to me that I was a virgin when I married, and Jack respected that.

He isn't religious in any way, but he never minded me saying my prayers every night. I would lie on my back with my hands cupped, then blow down my top, three times, which was a habit we'd learnt as children. I said the *kalmah*, the Holy Prayer; then the *kalmah-sherif*, then I'd go off into my own prayers, still in Urdu. I'd ask God to keep us safe, to give us a roof over our heads, to show us the right way forward. If we were travelling I'd ask Him to keep us out of danger on the road. I'd pray that we wouldn't be caught up with by my brothers or the bounty hunter, that one day we'd be free. Then I'd pray for Jack's family back home and for the individual members of my family. That God would look after them, and not bring them to harm; above all, that He would not let any of them die before I could say a final goodbye. Then I'd ask Him to change the feelings in their hearts, so that they would come to see that what we'd done wasn't wrong but what was meant to be.

Jack totally respected my beliefs, and remained intrigued by the whole subject of Islam. Quite a few of the discussions we had during the long hours we spent in these bed and breakfast rooms were about religion. I told him about the Prophet and his journey to Mecca; how the fasts and festivals fitted in with that; about the principles that told people within Asian communities how to behave towards each other; how one of the five tasks of Islam is to help the poor; how people in Asian communities feel duty-bound to help each other in times of hardship: things that were meat and drink to me but unknown, at that time, to him.

I even started teaching him Urdu. Just a few simple phrases and sentences at first, such as, 'Hello', 'Goodbye', 'How are you?' I was amazed at how quickly he picked it all up, how well those words sounded on his lips.

After ten days in Sandown we had another appointment with Brenda Steele at her office in Newport, to sort out the details of our wedding. Her organization had found the £75 for the licence, and now a date had to be set; for some legal reason we were to be married on the island instead of on the Mainland, and we had to have spent three weeks on the island before the appointed day.

We were very excited. Even if we were still on the run, our forthcoming marriage was going to legitimize our love at last, make it impossible that I could be snatched back and forced to marry Bilal.

Brenda Steele seemed rather less friendly than she had been before. 'Well,' she said briskly, 'this is the date that's been arranged for you. I've got a driving lesson at two o'clock that afternoon so you're going to have to pick a time to fit in with that.'

I looked over at Jack and thought: The most important event of my life and we're going to have to fit it round her driving lesson.

'That's how it's going to have to be done,' Brenda

132

insisted, when I protested, 'because I'm going to have to be one of the witnesses.'

I felt sad, and hurt. You would have thought another woman would understand what a special day it was for me, particularly after everything we'd been through in order to get married. But I decided to put these thoughts to the back of my mind. The main thing was that the wedding was going ahead; I didn't want anything to ruin that.

So we went down to the registry office to meet the registrar. Brenda had given him our real names, which we thought at the time was a bit odd because originally we were going to have to be taken off the island.

'Don't worry, love,' Jack said, 'they can hardly marry us in false names. It wouldn't be valid. But I'm sure they've got their plan well worked out.' We didn't question it further because we both trusted this women's refuge group entirely. We didn't want to seem difficult, and we were deeply grateful for everything they were doing for us.

With the date set, I said to Jack that it would be wonderful if I could have a new dress for my big day. Obviously we didn't have a huge budget, but there was a small sum left over from his clothing grant. In the end I found a navy-blue dress in a secondhand shop in Sandown High Street. It had chiffon sleeves, one of which was ripped, so we got it for a special price of £10. After we'd bought it I cut the torn sleeve off at the bottom and stitched the rest of the rip up. It looked terrific. Then I had a really nice pair of black shoes – the pair I'd brought from home specially for the occasion and that I'd been carefully carting around ever since.

I lay awake half the night before. I wanted friends and bridesmaids to make a fuss of me, a sister to share my private thoughts and excitement, brothers to organize, a mother to supervise, a loving father to give me away. As I tried to sleep in that little room I thought of all I was missing out on; what might have been if things had only been different, if my family had somehow been able to accept us, or if Jack had somehow been the supposedly right person for me and I could have had a grand traditional wedding like Miriam's.

The next thing I knew, it was morning – my wedding morning! We got washed and dressed and had our breakfast. On the front doorstep Jack gave me a hug and a kiss and told me everything would be all right. I knew I'd drastically lost weight and was as skinny as a pole, but he still told me how beautiful I looked in my special dress.

Then we walked up together to the bus stop. As a child I'd dreamed of six white horses and a fairytale glass coach, and here we were standing in the March wind waiting for a green Isle of Wight double-decker bus. But I was marrying the man I loved, who loved me enough to risk his life for me; and that was worth all the glass carriages in the world.

At the registry office in Newport we sat and waited, it seemed for hours, all dressed up with a stomach full of butterflies.

Finally Brenda Steele turned up late from her driving lesson, with Kelly, another lady who worked for the women's refuge group. We went inside and trooped upstairs to a big room that smelt strongly of the polish they obviously used on the gleaming wooden floor. They had this lovely music playing and it brought tears to my eyes because the place was so empty. I wanted to see the smiling faces of family and friends, the flash of the photographer's camera, the throwing of rice and hugs of congratulation. We hadn't even had enough money to buy ourselves wedding rings, so the registrar agreed to do the ceremony without them.

We were just into the service when all of a sudden Jack started laughing. A little at first, but then suddenly he was in hysterics. He could not stop. It was the same kind of laughter I'd had that first night in Huddersfield – just nerves. But I could see the registrar was getting impatient with it, because he had to interrupt the service about three times. Brenda Steele did not look amused.

Finally Jack got control of himself and we solemnly said our vows. For me, it was a perfect moment. All that we'd been through suddenly seemed justified. I'd done it! Now I was Jack's wife, and I would devote the rest of my life to looking after him. We signed our names in the register and made our way back down to the main entrance doors. Brenda gave us each a big hug and congratulated us. Then she said, 'You do realize you're going to have to leave the island now. On Monday.'

'What d'you mean? Why?'

'Because you've been married in your real names.'

We stood there in total shock. We couldn't take it in.

'But . . .' Jack began. Then: 'I thought – I thought the plan was that—'

Brenda didn't even let him finish. 'I'm sorry,' she said. 'It's going to be too big a risk for you to stay.'

She gave us no further time, no further reasons, just turned round as if nothing had happened, said goodbye, and strode off. Her colleague gave us this sort of 'I'm sorry' shrug and followed.

Words can't explain the awful fear that went through me then. Brenda had given us no explanation of why we had to leave, and there'd been not a shred of understanding in her voice – of what it felt like to be told to quit this place that had become such a haven for us.

Back in Sandown at the B and B we shared a plateful of salmon pâté sandwiches and fell into bed. I'd always dreamed that my wedding night would be such a beautiful, intimate occasion, finally giving myself physically to the man I loved. But we were so shocked by this news, and so scared, that all we could think about was what might happen now.

Jack held me tight and told me not to worry, that he'd work something out, that it would be all right. I fell asleep that night, my wedding night, trembling and in tears.

11

It wasn't until almost a year later that we discovered why they'd thrown us off the island like that. You might wonder why we didn't stand up to Brenda Steele and ask her what the hell was going on. Or tell her we were staying on the island anyway. But at that time we had a severe case of what you might call 'standing on your head syndrome'. If somebody had come up to us and said, 'Right, you two, go and stand on your heads in the corner of that room,' we'd have replied, 'How long for?' We were just so screwed up we didn't know whether we were coming or going. And the fact was that they had married us in our real names. The certificate said, *Newport, Isle of Wight.* After what had happened in Grimsby we couldn't run the risk of staying. But it was the hardest thing we'd yet had to do, saying goodbye to that beautiful island.

One moment everything was getting sorted out. We were going to be married. We were going to have a place to live. We were surrounded by supportive people in this place where Zena had no relatives and where we felt completely safe. The next moment there we were, back to square one, on the bloody road again.

We left, as instructed, on the Monday morning. We never spoke to Brenda or Emma again, we just packed and went. We had to take the bus over to the DSS first thing to pick up our remaining money, so by the time we'd got on the hovercraft and over to Portsmouth it was late afternoon. We didn't have a clue where we were going: north, east, or west – or how we were going – so we decided we'd better stop at least for the night in Portsmouth. We had only forty pounds left, so our priority was to head to the DSS, get a list of places that did housing benefit, and try to find somewhere to stay.

But when we eventually located the social security offices near the Guildhall, the queue stretched halfway round the outside of the building. There was only half an hour left till they closed.

'This is no good,' I said to Zena, 'we're going to have to get the *Yellow Pages* and start cold-calling a few places.' I had an idea that if we could just get in somewhere for the night we could try to persuade the landlord to take housing benefit, as we'd done in Grimsby.

Booking was the easy bit. 'Oh yes, we've got a room,' came the answer from the first place we called. We found our way over there and it seemed really nice, a big Victorian house with a long flight of steps up to the front door. We knocked and this well-dressed lady answered it. 'Oh, I'm so sorry,' she said, as soon as she saw us, 'I've just realized there's been an overbooking and the room's taken.'

I knew from the way she was looking at us that she was lying, but what could I do? Whether it was because we were mixed race or in such a shabby state I don't know. But there was no point arguing about it. I just thought: Right, on we go.

So we went and found another telephone box and booked up another place. By the time we got there we were completely shattered. This burly bloke opened the front door, took one quick glance at us, said, 'Room's gone,' and slammed the door in our faces. I was so angry I felt like kicking it down, going in and saying, 'Hold on a minute, what is your bloody *problem* here? We've got the money, we can give it to you up front.' But Zena was tugging at my arm. 'Come on, Jack, just leave it, we'll find another one.'

Eventually I got us booked into a third place. The landlady's name was Mrs Grime, which perhaps should have warned us. The house was another of these large Victorian places, but even from the outside this one looked putrid. The windows were filthy and through the spattered dirt you could see torn, nicotine-stained net curtains. But it was after eight o'clock, and I was determined we were going to get our heads down, no matter what.

We rang the bell and this woman opened the door. She must have been in her late fifties. She had a large, mangy cat in one hand and was clearly half-cut. 'Oh yes,' she drawled, 'there's a room available. Though you're very lucky to get it because I had another couple booked in.' That I didn't believe. It was out of season and the place was so filthy you wouldn't have let your dog stay there. As we walked through the front door we were hit by this overpowering stench of cat piss. Just by the staircase was a large handwritten notice which read, NO ALCOHOL, NO DRUGS, NO GLUE SNIFFERS, NO PETS.

The room she showed us to was unbelievable. I've been in some dives in my time, but this topped them all. The wallpaper was stained with great brown patches and peeling off the wall in swathes. There were spiders' webs up by the cracked plaster. There were bugs and cockroaches among the dustballs on the carpet. I half expected to see David Attenborough crawling out from under the bed.

Down the hall the toilet looked as if it hadn't been cleaned in years. The seat was spattered with urine, the floor was awash with water; at least we hoped it was water. When Mrs Grime drew back the plastic curtain and showed us the shower cubicle I thought at first it had a marble-effect pattern on the floor. Then I realized it was a matted carpet of old hair.

I asked Mrs Grime whether she'd take housing benefit.

'What I'll do,' she replied, as she tottered from side to side and her cat made another desperate effort to escape, 'is I'll get you the form and you can fill it in for me. But you'll have to leave me money for the key and your electricity card.'

I could see from Zena's face that she didn't want to stay, but we couldn't go on.

'Look, love,' I said, pulling her into the room. 'We're not going to get anywhere else now. Don't look at it as a night, look at it as a few hours. We can get up early and scarper.'

'And not pay?'

'Yeah. There's no way I'm handing over forty quid for this dump. We'll sign the form so she can get her housing benefit, give her the key money and piss off.'

I went out and got us a bag of chips. We ate them in the room, then crashed out. We slept in our coats on top of the bed, with Zena's face pillowed in her Aran sweater. Neither of us fancied risking the sheets.

I woke up with the first light. 'Come on, love,' I whispered to Zena. We crept up, grabbed the bags and tiptoed out. I was worried that Mrs Grime might be the kind of serious lush who'd be up early for a top-up. But it was OK, the place was dead. Not even the cats were stirring. Soon we were safely down the steps and away into the morning. I had a little notebook with me and I remember writing in it, *47 St Botolph's Avenue, never ever again.*

We found a café and had the wash that we hadn't dare have in that filthy sink at Mrs Grime's. Then we sat over a pot of coffee and tossed a coin.

'Tails we go west. Heads east,' I said.

The coin spun round and round on the red Formica top and came down tails.

'West it is, then.'

We hadn't a clue which motorway to take, or how to get out there. So I nipped down to this taxi rank and asked how much it would be for a cab out to the slip road. Three or four quid, they said. We went for it.

The cab dropped us off and we stood there on the approach road to the M27 for a good three hours. There was a bitterly cold March wind. Zena had never hitched before and the enthusiasm she'd displayed when we first stood on the roadside with our thumbs out was fast waning. I rolled up my trousers and started dancing around like a mad idiot singing, 'Always look on the bright side of life'. I could see she was getting her first taste of hitchhiker's blues. Plus we were both shitting ourselves about being so exposed. Who knew who might be in the stream of cars driving past?

Eventually these two lads pulled up in a battered old Escort. They looked totally dodgy to me, but what the hell, they were going down to Poole, it was a lift.

'We're on a mission,' they said, laughing. I assumed by that that they meant some criminal deed, so I kept mum. 'Have you had a feed?' they asked, when we told them how long we'd been waiting.

'We had a coffee.'

'We ain't got a lot of cash on us at the moment, but you can have this quid if you want,' they said, passing us back a pound coin. 'Get you a roll and a pot of tea maybe.'

I was really touched by that because they were definitely both very salty dudes. It takes one to know one, as they say.

In Poole we went straight to Housing Benefit to try to organize ourselves a place to stay. These lads dropped us off near the office. In we went as usual and I asked for a private interview. We got given a booth and this moustachioed bloke appeared. Whether he was a racist, didn't like the look of us, or was just a professional jobsworth I don't know. But he'd certainly decided to give us a hard time from the word go. So we had no option but to take him through our story. He was definitely unimpressed. I explained what had happened in Grimsby. He wouldn't help us, he said, unless we put down our real names and NI numbers on the form.

'But we've been told,' I repeated, 'by the DSS officials in Grimsby that we mustn't do that for another three weeks. Until we're National Sensitive.'

'I'm sorry, you've got to give me more than that,' he was saying.

'But we've told you why we can't give you our real names . . .'

'Anyone who comes in here and wants our help has to fill in the forms correctly . . .'

He kept repeating stuff like that, and I was just sitting there thinking, All I want to do is deck this idiot, we've *told* him the story. In a last-ditch attempt to get him to help us I gave him PC Alan Jones's number in Lincoln. 'Ring this police officer,' I said, 'and he'll confirm who we are and what's happened.'

He went away. 'Yeah,' he said, coming back with his spectacles glinting officiously, 'I've had confirmation of what you've been telling me but you're still going to have to fill in the form. You can put those names you're going under, Michael and Sonya, but I'll need real parents' names and the real addresses of all the places you've stayed in over the last five years. And I must warn you that if you give false information you can be liable to prosecution.'

'Fair enough,' I replied, just to keep him quiet. When he'd gone, I said to Zena, 'Just write down any old shit, but try and remember what you've put in case he cross-questions us.' She wrote down a string of fictitious Asian names for her family and I came up with all these names and addresses in Dublin. (I think I thought it would take him longer to check with the Irish authorities.)

When he came back he leaned right over the counter towards me and chuckled. 'This name you've got here – Michael Burnley. You're from Burnley, aren't you, in Lancashire?'

'God, is it really that obvious?' I replied, playing dumb. If this is the way he wants it, I thought, let him think he's sussed it out. 'D'you think I should change it?' I went on.

'I don't know. You might be OK with it, but I'd say your accent gives you away slightly. I knew you were from that area, that town . . .'

141

'Right,' I said, going along with him. He was really chuffed about this. From the smile on his face he reckoned he was Columbo or something.

He looked over our forms and nodded. He seemed to have got what he wanted now. He gave us two bed and breakfast addresses and let us go. They were in East Bournemouth, a bus ride away. Like Grimsby and Cleethorpes, Poole and Bournemouth merge into each other, so it was hard to tell where one ended and the other began.

Zena:

When we got to East Bournemouth we were pleasantly surprised. The nearer of these two B and Bs this jobsworth man had given us was really nice. The hallways were tidy, the couple that ran it were friendly and welcoming. The room they showed us to, at the top, was like a converted attic, a bit dark but clean and comfortable, with a little shower cubicle in the room itself.

Although they were obviously OK for housing benefit, we had to put down thirty pounds of the money we had left as a deposit on the first night. That left us with only a couple of pounds, so that evening we made do for our evening meal with the free coffee sachets in the room and half a packet of cream crackers we had left from the island.

In the morning Jack headed down to the DSS to try to get us a crisis payment. But he met with the same resistance he'd had from Housing Benefit, that 'Michael Burnley' and 'Sonya Atkinson' weren't coming up on the computer. Telling an official our story in private made no difference. 'No,' they told him, 'you don't qualify for a crisis loan.'

He came home angry and empty-handed. We had no money at all. That evening our supper was a cup of coffee and one last cream cracker, shared between us. When we went to bed I wanted to close my eyes and never wake up again. As we lay there starving I said as much to Jack. 'I don't blame you,' he replied.

'I don't know what we're going to do, love,' he said, as we shared a cup of coffee in the morning. 'I really don't know what we're going to do.'

We decided eventually to try the Jobcentre. After the trouble we'd had at Housing and the DSS we weren't too hopeful of any joy with Unemployment, but it was worth a try. We hadn't the money for the bus so we walked across the long crescent of beach.

We were in luck. The Jobcentre manager, a Scouser called Craig Wilson, was brilliant, a truly sympathetic man. When we got into his private office and told him our story he was shocked. He picked up the phone and rang the DSS for us there and then. 'These two are genuine,' we heard him say. 'You've got to sort out a payment for them today.' We had no ID, nothing. He just took us at our word.

He explained that this stretch of coast, Bournemouth, Poole, down to Torquay, was a bit of a holiday destination for people on the dole. It was nicknamed Costa del Dole. He wasn't surprised, with our accents, that we were having problems claiming.

'It's a pity,' he said, 'that I haven't got the money to send you over to Jersey.' There was work going there, he knew. But they don't have social security on the Channel Islands, so we'd have had to have enough money to get there and live till Jack could find a job and get paid.

So we went back to the DSS and they issued us with an emergency grant. It was three days' money – about thirty or forty quid. We had to put most of it aside to cover the shortfall between what we were going to get from Housing and the actual cost of the B and B room. But it left us enough to stock up on essential supplies. Bread, marge, salmon pâté, instant coffee, powdered milk.

When we got back to the B and B that night Jack looked very pale all of a sudden. 'I feel a bit ill,' he said.

'It's only because you haven't had anything to eat, love,' I reassured him. He'd probably caught a chill, I thought, after our standing hitching in the cold wind. That would have been made worse by him not eating. I made us some sandwiches and a pot of tea and he fell into bed.

But when I woke up the next morning he couldn't open his eyes. He was just lying there, like a corpse, not even able to speak. I lifted up his arm and it just fell back. I didn't know what to do. We had no medical records with us and I was terrified that if we tried to see a doctor they'd insist on getting in touch with Jack's GP back at home, who was an Asian man. I didn't think I could take that risk.

So for four days I sat in our room and nursed him myself. The only medical supplies I had were Paracetamol and Lemsip. For two days he ate nothing, then he managed a dry cracker or two. I was living on custard creams.

By the fifth day I'd run out of supplies. I had a shower and got dressed to go out. I picked up a little tourist map of Bournemouth from the rack downstairs at the B and B and headed off. I felt terribly scared and alone, out in this strange town with Jack lying flat out sick in our room.

I found a little shopping precinct with a Spar shop, bought some more Lemsips and Paracetamols, salmon pâté and bread. Walking back, I decided it couldn't go on like this, I had to get help.

But I couldn't go to the doctor. Nor did I feel I could go to the landlady of the B and B. I thought that if she knew our story she might worry about the danger to herself and the other guests and throw us out. (She had kids; I would have completely understood if that had been her attitude.)

Obviously I couldn't phone my family.

I couldn't phone Jack's: from his phone calls home I knew his mother had relapsed into illness again and I didn't want to be blamed for upsetting her further. None of them had any money anyway, so how could they have helped?

I decided that my only hope was to try Victim Support in Lincoln, the lady who'd been such a help in sorting us out with the Isle of Wight – Margaret Jackson.

'It's Sonya Atkinson here,' I said, when I finally got through.

'Yes.'

'Jack – you know – Michael's fallen very ill. We need your help.'

'What's wrong with him?' It was the same woman, but she sounded different – busy, uninterested.

'I don't know,' I said. 'He's just lying flat out in bed with his eyes closed. I'm terribly worried about him.'

'Can't you get a doctor to him?'

I explained about the medical records and about our doctor being Asian.

'Look, I'm sorry, Sonya,' came her voice. 'You're out of our area now, there's nothing much I can do for you. If you want any more help from us you'll have to go up to London to Head Office.'

'Who would I speak to there?'

'I don't have any names, you'd just have to go up there.'

'I can't get him to London. He's sick. Anyway, we don't have the money for the fare.'

'I'm sorry, Sonya, you're on your own.' And she put the phone down, as abruptly as that. I was dumbfounded. I must have stood there for a good ten seconds just staring at the receiver. She'd seemed so friendly and supportive before. At the coach station she'd hugged me and told me to keep in touch. There had been tears in her eyes. What was going on?

I ran back upstairs to Jack. He was just the same, eyes closed like a corpse.

I sat there beside him and tried to tell him what she'd said, but he could hardly open his eyes. He couldn't take it in. He just groaned vaguely and mumbled.

I began to cry. I felt so helpless. I must have sat there sobbing for hours. I really thought he was going to pass away; that this was the end of it.

This is all my fault, I thought. I should never have got up and gone round to his house that morning. I should never have done it. I should have accepted my lot and stayed where I belonged.

What have I done?

I put my hands together. 'Please God,' I prayed, 'surely this wasn't meant to be. Please please God, make him better.'

JACK:
I don't know to this day what that illness was. It must have been nervous exhaustion, I think. It was as if my mind had just said, 'OK, mate, that's enough. You're not going any further for the time being.'

I remember that first morning trying to open my eyes. It sounds disgusting but they were just sealed up with sleep. Zena had to bathe them to get them open.

After a few days I started to recover. Zena had drawn a blank with Margaret Jackson of Victim Support so as soon as I had the strength I decided I'd phone PC Alan Jones.

'I'm in a terrible state,' I told him. 'We can't go any further.'

'I'm sorry, Michael,' he replied. 'There's really nothing I can do for you from here. There's nobody I can tell you to go and see. It's a different county, a different lot. If I was more senior, mate, possibly. Sorry.'

As he was to say later, he was just a foot soldier. His heart was in the right place, but his powers were limited.

We'd run out of money again. Most of our crisis payment had gone straight to the B and B, so we were down to nothing. We literally didn't have a penny in the world. I didn't know what to do. I had this little brass zippo lighter that I thought I might be able to sell for a quid or so in a junk shop. A quid would get us a pot noodle and some more crackers.

But I couldn't get anyone to give me cash for it. Right, I thought, I'm going down to the church at the bottom of the road. I had a vague idea that there might be a priest there who could help us. In my childhood churches used to do food parcels. They were Spam and stuff that Zena wasn't allowed to eat, but there might be bread or chocolate in there as well. Something to keep us from total starvation.

But the church doors were locked. I remember turning away from them and standing leaning against this old stone wall and looking at the row of shops over the road. It was the first time since I'd left home that I'd honestly thought I might crack on with something. Nick some gear, do a snatch – anything to get us something to eat. I was just standing there thinking that, yes, despite Zena's disapproval, despite the risk of getting caught, it really had come to it, when this doddery old white-haired fellow came up to me. 'Have you been trying to get in them church gates?' he asked. Here we go, I thought, a reprimand: this is all I bloody need.

'If you're looking for the priest,' he went on, 'he lives down there.' He pointed to the road on the right. 'That end house, with the Elizabethan timbers.'

Well, if that isn't the sign from God, I thought, I don't know what is. I walked down the road, knocked on the door and who should open it but two police officers. The priest had just been burgled!

'If you've come to see Father Devlin,' said one of the coppers, 'you'll have to wait here a minute, lad.' I thought to myself, *This cannot be happening*.

The Old Bill left and the priest came out. He was a lovely old boy, a traditional Catholic father, dressed in the long black cassock. He invited me into his front room, sat me down, and asked how he could help. So I began to tell him our story. He was sitting there nodding and running his finger over his jaw and I could see I was wearing him down. He'd just been burgled, poor bloke, and now I'd landed on his doorstep. He had to be thinking this was a test of his faith.

147

'Look,' he said eventually, 'if I give you a tenner, will that see you?'

I've cracked it, I thought. 'That'd be marvellous, father,' I replied.

So he gave me the money. 'I'll definitely pray for you, my son,' he said as he showed me out. I need it, I thought. I'd been just a whisker away from slipping back into crime.

Zena's going to be made up about this, I said to myself, as I stopped at the supermarket and bought us a cannelloni. She was. Delighted. It was the first proper hot meal we'd had in ages. The landlady allowed us to microwave it in her kitchen.

A couple of days later a letter arrived for us, out of the blue. It was on DSS-headed notepaper, from one Dennis Baird, who signed himself as a senior officer with the DSS in Lincolnshire. 'Dear Mr Burnley,' it read:

I've been informed of your situation and am urgently trying to contact my colleagues in Newcastle to secure your names as positively National Sensitive.

I'm sorry to hear of your circumstances. If I can be of help in any way, please do not hesitate to call me either here at the office, or at home (numbers above). Any call will of course be treated in the strictest confidence.

Yours sincerely,
Dennis Baird

I read this downstairs in the B and B lounge, then ran up to Zena. 'Look at this.'

'What is it?'

I showed her.

'What does he want from us?'

'No, love, he's offering to help us.'

'How does he know we're here?'

I could only assume that he'd been passed the letters we'd written to DSS Headquarters from the Isle of Wight, formally applying for National Sensitive status. Being in the senior position he was, he must, presumably, have had access to details of all claims; including the addresses of claimants. And we had told both Margaret Jackson and PC Alan Jones that we were in Bournemouth. But after what had happened in Grimsby, Zena was obviously worried about the security aspect of this letter turning up on our doorstep.

'Don't worry,' I reassured her. 'This is a very senior officer. "Any call",' I read, ' "will be treated in the strictest confidence. I am sorry to hear of your circumstances." He's moving to secure our names as National Sensitive. It's OK.'

'Are you sure?'

'Yes, love. There's no way this would be on the main computer.'

I immediately phoned both telephone numbers. There were answerphones on both, but I had a really good gut feeling about this letter. Could it be, I wondered, as I read and re-read it, that our luck was finally changing?

That same afternoon we took a walk into the centre of town. We'd received our next giro and needed to replenish our supplies. We were coming down the steep pedestrian precinct from the city centre when Zena suddenly froze.

'What is it?' I said, instantly switching into red-alert mode.

'Down there,' she said. Beyond the bollards, about a hundred yards away, was a blue Toyota Corolla full of Asian guys.

'It isn't them, is it?'

'I don't know, Jack.' She looked petrified.

'Come on,' I said. And we just ran for it, up the street, across the central park, along the seafront to our B and B.

'D'you think it *was* them?' I asked, when we were safely back in our little room.

'I don't know, love. But one of them looked exactly like my uncle Sulman.'

'Did he see you?'

'I don't think so.' She sat there by my side, on the bed, breathless. 'We've got to get out of here,' she said.

We couldn't risk staying. I wasn't so much worried about Dennis Baird's letter, which I felt sure was secure, as the fact that with us having got married on the Isle of Wight in our real names either her brothers or the private investigator might easily have traced us there. Once they'd established we'd been there they would probably have figured that we'd be likely to go along the coastline either east or west. After Southampton, Bournemouth was the first big place west. We'd been there almost a fortnight now. Even if it hadn't been her uncle in the car we had to move on.

From the outside our reaction might make us seem paranoid, but after Grimsby and the inexplicable events of the Isle of Wight we were ready for just about any eventuality. Every time there's a knock at the door your pulse quickens, not knowing who it is. Every time the phone rings, as you're picking it up and saying 'Hello' you're thinking, Is this them? Have they finally found us? Is this another trick call to lure us to a rendezvous where we'll meet our deaths? When you're walking in the street and a car slowly pulls up at the side of you, you try not to freeze, as the palms of your hands begin to sweat, your breathing becomes rapid, your heart starts beating nineteen to the dozen. Is this someone just innocently asking for directions? Or could it be your executioner wanting to make sure it's you before he grabs you and pulls you into the car?

After a while it's so easy to slip into a false sense of security. You've been so long on the road and it hasn't happened yet. Maybe the threat has diminished. Maybe they've given up. But that's the point at which you've got to jolt yourself and think, Right, how would I handle it now if that door suddenly flew open? How would I react? Where would I move? How would I protect Zena? Which is our escape route?

You do think like that, and you've got to think like that. How else can I describe how it feels? Imagine yourself with a death threat hanging over you. What background noise was that that you just ignored? Which door should you have double-checked to make sure it's locked? Which window could they easily smash through? Where would you run if they did burst in in ten seconds' time?

Imagine your senses jumping like that all day, every day. All night, every night. Then you'll start to understand how we were feeling, and how we still feel. Maybe we have over-reacted, maybe it is paranoia, but then, in a way, paranoia has become a friend to us, because it's kept us safe. So far.

The next big place along the coast was Torquay, so in the morning I went back up to the Jobcentre and asked Craig Wilson if he wouldn't mind booking us an appointment at the Torquay DSS, so that this time we wouldn't have all the hassle we'd had on our arrival in Bournemouth. I had an idea he might be able to say something to them, too. Make the path a little smoother for us.

Before we left we tried phoning Dennis Baird one last time. Both of his answerphones were still on. Then we paid the B and B landlady and caught the bus out to the approach road to the main A31.

It was another loweringly cloudy March morning and after we'd been standing there with our thumbs out for an hour or two the heavens opened in a torrential downpour. We were both absolutely soaked. Zena's khaki cotton coat was hanging off her. Her hair was stuck round her face. She looked at me like a drowned rat and shouted, 'I'm not bothered where we go! I don't care if we never get to fucking Torquay! When we get to the next town we're stopping, I'm not going on, I'm not putting up with this any more!'

She was hysterical. It was the first time she'd ever screamed at me like that. I did my best to calm her down, all the while knowing that it's when it's raining that lifts are hardest to come by. The sign we'd made saying TORQUAY had run into an inky mess.

Luckily, after only a few more minutes of standing there a battered Skoda splashed to a halt and this middle-aged gent wound down his window and asked where we were going. He could, he said, take us some of the way. He was a prison officer. It turned out that he'd just had a massive row with his wife and was out driving to calm himself down. This is all we need, I thought – someone else with problems. But I soon realized that this was a good thing: the more he talked the further we were going. And it was quite fascinating stuff. Both he and his new wife had kids from their previous marriages and they weren't getting on. Then they had two houses between them, in separate counties, and couldn't agree which one to sell. And so on. We just listened and I murmured 'Right' or 'Yeah' from time to time, and he drove us further and further west. When he got particularly heated his foot would go down harder on the accelerator. Well, I thought, this is a pretty good arrangement. He wants therapy and we want the lift. Before we knew it he'd driven us seventy or eighty miles.

He dropped us off finally outside a Little Chef in a dank green valley in the middle of nowhere. We had just enough money left for a pot of coffee. So we sat and shared that, taking it in turns to nip in and use the hand dryer in the toilets to dry ourselves off. At one point I was balanced halfway up the wall with one foot in the sink and one foot on this upside-down wastepaper bin. In walked this huge bloke with a beard, took one look at me and went, 'Bloody hell!'

'It's all right, mate, I'm just trying to get my coat dry.'

He was laughing so much he could hardly pee.

Outside on the road I was trying to keep Zena's spirits up. 'This is it,' I said, 'this is the last leg. We'll definitely get a lift all the way to Torquay.'

'No, we won't.'

'Right,' I said finally, pulling out a pair of sunglasses I'd bought on the Isle of Wight. 'I'm going to put on my magic glasses and as soon as I've put them on a car will stop.' I was only fooling around but it was weird. As I put them on this lorry screeched to a halt beside us.

'Bloody hell!' I said, taking them off again. 'That was quick.'

The driver was a burly guy called Carl. Amazingly enough, he was going to a place six miles outside Torquay.

'So what are you doing down here?' he asked, as we drove off. Oh well, we said, we were just hitching along the South Coast, doing a spot of travelling, but we'd run out of money. Did he know of any cheap places to stay in Torquay?

'I wish I'd met you two a week ago,' he said. 'I had a beautiful place out in the country. You could have had that. Me and the wife parted company recently, so it's empty. But it's no good now because all the gas and electricity has been cut off. But I do know somebody in Torquay who might put you up. My boss.' He grinned. 'He runs a B and B.'

After he'd dropped his delivery off at an airport just outside town he pulled up at a phone box. 'Right,' he said, returning to the van with a big smile, 'you're fixed up.'

He didn't have time to take us all the way there so he dropped us at a bus stop. From there, he said, it was a short, direct ride into the centre.

As he said goodbye he pulled out a fiver. 'Take it,' he said. 'Maybe it'll get you a feed tonight.'

One thing this whole horrible experience has taught me is the truth of that saying, 'There's good and bad everywhere.' There is, and we'd been lucky at that point of damp desperation to have met one of the good ones. Those magic glasses had worked better than I could ever have imagined.

12

ZENA:
So Carl left us and we got on to this little Hoppa bus which was so completely packed with people we had to sit with our wet bags piled on our laps. It seemed as if I could hear every single thing that was happening in there; from the old ladies gabbling away down the front to the hectic crowd of teenage kids standing around us at the back, all shouting their heads off and laughing.

'I'm going out with so-and-so tonight.' 'I'm doing this.' 'I'm doing that.' *Hee-hee-hee-hee*. I just wanted to scream at the lot of them, 'Shut the fuck UP!' My nerves were that much on edge now.

What with the delay and Torquay being further than we'd thought, we were now late for the interview that Craig Wilson had set up for us at the DSS. When we got to the town centre we hurried straight there but our excuses were not accepted.

'I'm sorry, you can't see anybody now,' the woman on reception told us. 'You should have got here in time for your appointment.'

'But we've got no money,' we said. 'We had to hitch to get here.' That didn't interest her. There was no way, she said, we could get a crisis payment or even an interview; we'd have to come back the next day.

There was nothing for it but to head off, praying that Carl's promise of a B and B would come good. When we found the place the boss was out but his wife was there. She seemed nice enough in her long A-line skirt and loose flowery blouse: cheerful and talkative.

'Oh yes,' she said, 'I got Carl's message. We've got a room for you.'

It was another pleasant place: a big rambling house on a street corner, full of clean if rather box-like little rooms. Being out of season she seemed glad of the extra cash, even if it was through Housing Benefit. She took us up to the first floor, a room at the front overlooking the street.

Carl's boss Duncan was quite strange, a weird mixture between smarmy and annoyingly inquisitive. Almost as soon as we came down to the lounge that evening (there were no tellies in the rooms) he'd started on the personal questions. Where did we come from in the north, where had my father *originated* from, and so on. I couldn't be doing with it; I didn't want to answer questions like that. I was tired, hungry, and sick of the whole bloody thing. I just wanted someone to reach out and help us.

During our stay he'd come in when we were sitting in the lounge, say, 'Hello' or 'Everything all right?' and then just stand there and stare at us, as if he was expecting us to say something. More than once I was on the verge of saying, 'Oh, just leave me alone!'

It wasn't only that I was terribly tense – I was so *tired*. It had got to a point where I couldn't remember things I'd said. Duncan would ask me a question and I'd make up some answer just to keep him quiet; the next day he'd ask it again and I'd think, Oh no, what did I tell him yesterday?

'Where do you come from, love?'

'Up north.'

'Which part of the north?'

'Erm, I come from Tilsley.' (Tilsley's a little village on the outskirts of our city.)

'Oh, right.'

Then he'd ask me the same question the next day and I wouldn't be able to remember exactly what I'd told him. So I'd say nothing. Then he'd say, 'Oh well,' and stand there staring at me as if I was an idiot; for not remembering where I was supposed to live.

But we were both feeling totally screwed up. Sometimes, sitting upstairs in our room, we'd quiz each other just to try and keep ourselves sane.

'Where are you from?'

'West Yorkshire.'

'Who are you?'

'Sonya Atkinson.'

'What are you going to be doing this afternoon?'

'Stepping out to the Spar shop.'

And so on, with the most trivial details.

Downstairs again Duncan would come in while we were watching TV and start running Carl down. We didn't want to hear that, because Carl had been nothing but a good angel to us. But Duncan would stand there and say, 'I don't know whether I should really be keeping him on.' Carl had spent too much time doing this; or he was no good at that. 'Oh yeah, right,' I'd mumble, just to shut him up.

Then he'd start going on about how he was having his boss round for dinner.

'Oh right,' I'd say. 'OK, then.'

He'd go on and on about this boss and the elaborate meal that he and his wife were preparing for him. It was the last thing either of us wanted to hear about. Torquay DSS had refused us a crisis payment and, once again, we were bloody starving. The hunger got so bad some days that we took to going to bed in the afternoon to avoid it. Once you were asleep you wouldn't feel the pangs.

When Duncan wasn't there his wife would come in. She was even more talkative than him.

'Oh, hello,' she'd say; then, 'I cook a really good curry.'

'Oh, right,' I'd reply, 'do you?'

'How d'you cook a curry, then?' she'd go.

Oh, *please*, I'd think. I really don't want to talk about food, especially not curry. I didn't want to be reminded of the delicious rogan joshes and biryanis Miriam used to make for us all every night. So I used just to click off when she was talking because I couldn't bear it. The smell from this woman's kitchen was enough to drive you mad in any case. She was forever frying. We'd sit upstairs without the telly to get away from it. But when we passed the door on our way out there was no avoiding it.

There was a bakery just down the street, too. The smell of that freshly baked bread just used to tug straight at my throat and stomach. Sometimes I'd be mesmerized by it. I'd stand there looking at the display and think: If I got arrested for walking in and picking up a loaf and just tearing it up and eating it now in the shop I wouldn't care.

JACK:
They were a very odd family altogether. There was a set of drums and an electric organ in the lounge, and every evening they'd all suddenly appear, Mum, Dad and the teenage kids, and start practising this song, right next to us as we were watching TV. It was an Andrew Lloyd Webber tune, something from *Phantom of the Opera*, and their rendition of it was truly terrible.

Maybe it was just the way we were feeling. Day after day after day we'd sat together in those dingy bed and breakfast rooms. Huddersfield, Cleethorpes, Grimsby, Lincoln, Sandown, Bournemouth, now here. Sometimes they all seemed to merge into one, with their ill-fitting furniture, their ancient TV sets, their sagging mattresses, their dreary decor and curtains. I was all set to become a wallpaper designer, the number of patterns I had stared at. Certainly they all smelt the same, that pukey mix of fag ash and stale sweat, overlaid with the sickly-sweet pong of air freshener and cleaning fluid.

We really sank to the depths in Torquay. Physically and mentally, we were both just absolutely drained. We didn't have a clue where we were going, who might help us, whether we'd *ever* get help, and if we did whether it would turn out to be yet another false start.

The morning after we arrived in Torquay we went back

up together to the DSS to make another claim. Once again they wanted our real names and NI numbers. Once again we tried to explain why we couldn't give them out. And once again I asked for a private interview with a senior manager.

The young woman at the reception desk wasn't buying this at all. The fact that Craig Wilson had set up the interview seemed to count for nothing. She refused to contact him. She refused to call PC Alan Jones. She refused to help at all.

All of a sudden I'd had enough. 'Right,' I said. 'Fair enough.' I got to my feet and walked out, Zena running in my wake wanting to know what the hell I thought I was doing.

'We're getting nowhere,' I told her. 'I'm going to try Dennis Baird again.'

We marched round the corner, found a phone box, called Baird's office number. Somebody upstairs must have been looking after us because this time I got straight through.

'Oh,' I began, 'hello, it's Michael Burnley, I've received your letter and—'

'Thank God you called,' came this voice. 'I've had your messages at home but I'm afraid I was away at a conference. I tried to get you at your bed and breakfast in Bournemouth but they said you'd just left . . .'

I explained what had happened – and the problem we currently faced with the DSS. 'I'm outside the office now,' I said. 'In fact I've just walked out because I cannot make them understand about us waiting to be National Sensitive—'

'I'll stop you right there,' Dennis Baird interrupted. 'Give me the name of the person you've been talking to.' She was just one of the women on reception – I couldn't remember her name.

'Don't worry,' he said. 'Give me half an hour and I'll call you back at that payphone.' So I gave him the number and we just stuck tight in the phone box and waited. I had started raining outside, and I remember staring out over these black railings at a bed of daffodils in this little park, hoping to God Baird could sort something out for us. My only cause for optimism was that this man's voice had sounded very strong and authoritative.

Sure enough, after half an hour or so the phone rang and it was Dennis Baird. 'Right,' he said, 'if you want to go back into that office now, I've arranged for you to see a fellow called Brian Dunstable. He's an ex-copper, but he's now working in the DSS. I've briefed him on your situation and he'll make sure you're properly looked after.'

We were to call him later, at home, Baird said, and let him know how it had all gone. So we went back in there and the transformation was miraculous. This difficult young lady had turned into someone who said, politely, 'Yes, if you'd just like to go down there into Room Four, Mr Burnley, we'll make sure that you're seen straight away.'

Brian Dunstable appeared immediately. He was extremely courteous and helpful and explained that he'd heard of cases similar to ours. He fully understood how serious such a death threat was.

'Don't worry,' he said at the end of the interview, 'I'm going to get you sorted out with a crisis payment straight away.' Within half an hour we were given a handwritten giro.

So we were able to renew our supplies. Nothing fancy because again the bulk of the money had to be put aside to cover the shortfall between the nightly cost of the B and B and what we'd be granted from Housing Benefit.

That evening I phoned Dennis at home and had a lengthy chat with him. He wanted to know exactly what had happened on the Isle of Wight and he seemed very sympathetic to our case. Eager, if he could, to do more. He didn't know how else he could help us right now, he said, but I was to keep in touch with him constantly. If we had any more problems with the DSS I was to phone him immediately.

In fact he said, 'I'll give you my full rank and if you go into any DSS office, anywhere, quote my surname and which department I'm from and tell them if they need confirmation to contact me directly. I'm not having you messed around any more,' he went on, 'and if you are, I'm going to make sure that heads will roll.'

Now these seemed to me like words of pure light coming down this phone. At *last* we'd got someone, within the social security organization, who could speak on our behalf. After all the endless hassle we'd had, just to get enough cash to survive, this was like a dream come true.

ZENA:
One of the things Dennis Baird suggested, during one of these long phone calls with Jack, was that we should do something to change our appearances. Nothing as drastic as plastic surgery, but just something to make us less instantly recognizable.

Jack had already started a rough beard; during his illness he hadn't been able to shave, and since then he'd let his facial hair grow. Now he decided to shape it and make it more of a feature. He went down the corridor to the bathroom with my pair of sewing scissors; when he came back I just burst out laughing.

'My God,' I said, 'it's Abraham Lincoln!' His face was so sunk and elongated that his cheeks were all but touching each other inside – he really did look exactly like the famous president. As I continued to shriek with mad giggles on the bed he just swivelled round on his heel and vanished through the door. When he came back he was clean-shaven. My laughter had defeated him!

The one thing that really stood out about my appearance was my hair. It was so thick and black and it went right down below my bum. I could sit on it if I wanted to.

There were two problems with cutting it: one, we didn't have the money for a haircut, and two, in our Muslim religion you're not supposed to have your hair cut, ever. Over and above that, of course, was the fact that it had been long all my life and there was a part of me that really didn't want to lose it. But there was another side that was saying, Come on, it's going to have to go. If it's going to make you both safer it's got to be a good thing.

Jack discussed all this with Dennis Baird and Baird got rid of Objection One by offering to send down the money to have it done. Objection Two vanished when I thought hard about it and realized that this religious rule was really about vanity. In the circumstances the haircut was absolutely necessary.

'It'll grow again one day,' Jack said. He didn't want to see it go either.

So we found this little salon round the corner called Scruples. The hairdresser looked exactly like Andy Garcia, if a bit better groomed. He was certainly one of those men who know they're pretty good-looking.

'This is such beautiful hair,' he said, running his fingers through it. 'Why on earth are you having it cut?'

I looked at him and didn't know what to say. 'I just want a change,' I replied eventually, trying to laugh and sound lighthearted. 'I've had it like this for twenty-one years.'

'If that's what you want. But it seems an awful shame . . .'

I looked at Jack for reassurance. 'No, it's got to go,' I said.

'You're absolutely sure? I've had young girls jump up and run out screaming when they see what I've done.'

'No, no. I'm sure.'

Jack left and Andy showed me a book of styles. I chose a short bob. Now he wanted to take my photograph. 'Just a quick before-and-after shot,' he said.

No, no, I thought, I don't want that. They might put it up in the window. Who knew who might see it and know we were in Torquay?

161

'I'd really rather not,' I said.

'Oh, come on. It's only for my books. I've got a whole collection here of beautiful women with long hair.'

'No, no, you'd better not.'

I think he was starting to think I was a bit odd I was so persistent.

'It's only so I can show women when they come in what it'll look like afterwards,' he said.

Eventually I gave in and he took a photograph of me from the back, and one from the side but draped so you couldn't see my face.

Then he damped it down and got this huge pair of scissors. I could feel him gathering it up at the back. I was just about to turn round and say, 'No, leave it.' Then I thought, No, no, I've got to have it done.

Jack was pacing round the block outside. Every three minutes or so he'd come into view, checking on the progress of the haircut. This hairdresser was in hysterics at Jack's inquisitive face appearing at regular intervals at this big picture window. Eventually he left us to it.

I listened to the scissors slicing through my hair, which had never been cut since I'd had my head shaved, in the traditional way, the day after I was born. Then he pulled this bunch away and held it up for me to see. It was four foot long, in perfect condition. He bundled it up in front of me.

He did a lovely job on what was left. When he'd finished and I looked in the long mirror at the end of the shop I couldn't believe it.

'My God,' he said, 'doesn't it make you look young!' He was right, it took years off me. Over the couple of months we'd been travelling I felt like I'd aged half a lifetime; now I felt twenty-one again.

It was raining outside. Andy offered me an umbrella so I wouldn't ruin his handiwork. Then I ran back to Jack at the B and B.

JACK:

There I was upstairs in our room, glued to the window, waiting for Zena to come round the corner, wondering what it was going to look like. Eventually this woman turned the corner and it was only because she was wearing that distinctive khaki coat that I recognized her as Zena. She looked completely different.

'Where's the hair?' I asked.

'He kept it,' Zena said. 'He said he might use it to make some extensions.'

'You could have sold that,' I said. I was all ready to go back down there and get some money for it, but Zena stopped me. He'd done a lovely job, she said, and it had only cost her nineteen pounds. So we already had a tenner over from the thirty pounds Dennis had sent us.

'OK,' I said. 'We'll let it go.'

I suggested that we celebrate by treating ourselves to a really nice scran and then maybe step out for a drink as well. So we got ourselves a hot pie and chips each from a takeaway and took a stroll up to this little local pub. 'There won't be anybody in here at opening time,' I said. 'We should be OK.'

We were just having a quiet drink and a game of pool when these five Scousers came in. I was a bit wary of these lads at first. But they seemed amiable enough, putting their money down on the rim of the table for the next game. Perhaps I made a mistake in beating the shit out of them because when we were all gathered round having a drink and a chat afterwards (we'd got on to the thorny old topic of money) one of them suddenly said, 'These bloody Pakis have all the money these days, don't they?'

Here we go, I thought. This is it, this is where it goes up. I had this pool cue in my hand and I just let it slip gently round so I had the butt end of it ready. It was plain enough that Zena was Asian and quite possibly Pakistani and that I was with her.

I looked straight at him. '*What* did you say?' I asked.

Looking back I reckon he'd just come out with this stupid remark without thinking because he was immediately apologetic. And his mate turned on him and said, 'What the fucking hell did you say that for?'

'No,' he was saying, 'I didn't mean that ... What I was trying to say ...' He was attempting to back out of it and all the while digging himself deeper and deeper in.

'Listen, fellers,' said the barman, who was fortunately a big fellow. 'Pack it in.'

The subject was dropped. What I thought I was going to do with that pool cue I have no idea. At that time it was probably broader than I was. And there were five of them against one of me. But I remember thinking, You've got to make a show here. Because if you don't they're just going to dive in and we're going to get kicked to death here.

When it had calmed down we went over to the bar and I said quietly to Zena, 'We don't leave here till they're gone.' Otherwise, I thought, as soon as we go they're just going to finish up their drinks and come after us.

I don't think it was meant as that spiteful a dig. But he was, I'm quite sure, just testing the waters. I'm a great believer that if you act like a victim you become a victim. Bluff, in a case like that, is 99 per cent of it. If you show somebody that you're not prepared to be intimidated they'll back off. But if I hadn't made that stand they'd have started taking liberties, prolonged that racist stuff and made us feel, at the least, very uncomfortable.

It was also true to say that after two months on the road there was a real rage and frustration building up inside me. I was sick and tired of having doors slammed in our faces. People staring at us openly in the streets. Part of it was obviously that we looked like a pair of starvation victims from Ethiopia. But part of it also was that we were a mixed-race couple.

I'd never known discrimination before. Where I grew up my friends were from all kinds of backgrounds – black, brown, whatever. You can't say that I never noticed colour, because if you don't see the colour you don't see the person, but it had never made an ounce of difference to me.

I hate that sort of ignorance. Being on the receiving end of it, day after day, was really getting to me.

There'd been one evening in Bournemouth where we'd been walking along the front. Three elderly people on a bench had just stared openly at us. They were leaning forward so far I thought they were going to topple off. Zena always used to say, 'Just ignore it, ignore it.' But I couldn't. I went over to them and said, 'What the fucking hell are you lot staring at?' Then, of course, they looked away. Back home, in the old days, I'd never have done that. I'd have used my head and kept my thoughts to myself. Certainly to a benchful of old dears who could have been my mother. But my fuse was getting shorter.

So I reckon part of my eagerness to be ready with that pool cue was just a general build-up of undirected fury. I wanted to let off steam. I certainly wouldn't have been averse to getting stuck into that racist idiot.

Once again I felt very strongly that Zena was coming into my world. Because that sort of situation is what I've been brought up with. You learn how to deal with show-downs like that. Now Zena was learning it too.

ZENA:
I don't think that lad meant badly by using the word 'Paki'. I think it just slipped out, because afterwards he looked at me in a very contrite manner. 'I'm really sorry,' he said.

But I always call people weak-minded if they use words like that. They don't understand, half of them, what they're saying. They'll classify all kinds of different people with the same word: Indians, from all over the sub-continent, of all castes, Pakistanis the same, Hindus, Sikhs . . .

I can never understand why they can't see that we'd find such a word insulting. I'd never use such a rude word to a white person. The problem is that in the communities these people are brought up in such words are used all the time. They never try to broaden their horizons by going out and meeting other cultures; if they did they'd soon realize why it was offensive to say such things.

I hated being stared at in the street just as much as Jack did. People sometimes even pointed a finger at me; to the point where I'd think, Have I got two heads, or what? Looking back on it, I think it was because where we were, down south, on the coast, there were very few Asian people. So I was a novelty, especially being with Jack. But when people repeatedly point at you, you start to feel like, 'Why am I so different? I speak your language.' Sometimes people would even speak to me really slowly. 'How – are – you?' they'd go, as if I'd have problems understanding them. Boy, were they in for a shock!

Having my hair cut was a big step for me, another one down the long road from East to West. It had been strange enough for me just moving out of the traditional clothes I'd always worn at home to the Western stuff I had now. When I'd first started wearing skirts, on the Isle of Wight, I'd felt not just naked but also dirty in a way, as if I should rush home and cover myself up again.

JACK:
We continued to keep in touch with Dennis Baird. About a week after the Scousers incident he announced that he was going to come and pay us a visit. His daughter worked for a local rugby team and it just so happened that they were playing a Torquay side. So he was bringing her down anyway.

He arrived when we were having dinner – our favourite John West salmon pâté sandwiches. The phone rang and when I ran downstairs it was Dennis on the mobile, cruising the backstreets looking for our B and B.

I ran down and opened the front door for him. It was

as if someone had taken the balloon of my fantasy and stuck a pin in it. From the way he'd been speaking on the phone, the tone of his voice – 'Heads will roll' and all that – I'd imagined someone at least six foot, broad, muscular, impressive. Here before me stood this little chap of about five foot four, with glasses, who looked as if he needed a good meal. He wasn't shabbily dressed but, as Zena said later, you could tell he lived on his own.

'Dennis Baird,' he said, and held out a hand. My face must have given me away because he added, 'You were expecting someone totally different, weren't you?'

I laughed, and the ice was broken. He came up to our room and nibbled on a couple of our sandwiches, looking at them nervously as if they might very likely poison him.

He was obviously appalled at the state of us. As he said to me later, 'The only way I can describe it was that you looked as if you'd both crawled out of a plane crash. You just had this totally dazed look about you.'

Before he left he gave us a fiver. 'Try and get yourselves a proper meal, Michael,' he said. 'Even if it's just fish and chips. When I get back home I'm going to make some phone calls and see what we can get organized for you. I'll be in touch in the next couple of days.'

ZENA:

I didn't want to waste that five pounds Dennis had given us on just one hot meal. I'd spotted this little toasted-sandwich maker in the window of an Argos store in town. It cost nine pounds, so we put Dennis's money and four other pounds we'd saved together and bought it, along with a pack of cheese and a tin of baked beans.

This was like a mini-triumph for us. At last we could have regular hot meals, something other than the pâté sandwiches and pot noodles we'd lived on since we'd run away.

I'm not allowed to eat pork, which rules out a lot of cheap meats and spreads. We'd tried to vary the John West pâté, but after one jar of the beef flavour and one of the crab we'd returned eagerly to salmon! Otherwise, apart from crisp and chip sarnies and the odd takeaway, we'd not altered our diet, which was at least cheap.

Of course I hankered for variety, for the old days of regular, delicious meals. But that had to remain a distant dream, a situation I hoped I'd be in again one day. For the time being just allaying basic hunger was all we were concerned about.

You're not supposed to cook in B and B rooms, but this sandwich-maker was so small we used to plug it in and balance it on the window-ledge and then waft the smell out into the street with the palms of our hands. Anybody who'd seen us sitting there in the spring sunshine would have thought we were a right pair of nutters, worshipping this little machine, wafting away with our hands!

JACK:
True to his word, about three o'clock one afternoon a call came through from Dennis Baird. 'What I've managed to do,' he said, 'is have a word with the Torquay police. If you've got a pen handy take down these two names I'm going to give you.' They weren't particularly senior officers. One was a DCI, the other a DCS. 'If you have any trouble, with anything, give them a bell. They'll be there for you.'

He'd also managed to get us an appointment with some-one high up in Housing who was going to try and sort out something permanent for us in Torquay. Get us out of the B and B and into a place of our own.

Again, these were magic words coming down this phone. Someone was there, someone was taking an interest, some-one realized the seriousness of our situation – and they were going to *do* something. Things were starting to move.

'Right, Dennis,' I said, 'that's absolutely marvellous.'

'I'll be in touch with you in the next couple of days.'

But when he phoned back there was, he said, bad news.

'You know I told you that I'd made contact with those two police officers? I'm afraid their superior has taken it upon himself to ring up West Yorkshire to check you out.'

'In our real names.'

'He's used your real names, I'm afraid.'

'So now they know where we are. We're going to have to move again, we're going to have to get out.'

'I think you are.'

'What about the housing arrangements?'

'You'll have to forget it, Michael.' There was a long pause while I digested this information and my mind started spinning towards panic again. *Another move, another town, another nightmare with the DSS . . .*

'Listen,' Dennis Baird was saying, 'I'm going to come down there and fetch you, bring you back to Lincolnshire.'

'Honestly? D'you mean that?'

'Yeah. Don't worry. I've got to go down and see my other daughter in Plymouth anyway, so I'll pick you up on the way. I'll come by early tomorrow afternoon.'

13

JACK:
So around half past two the following day Dennis appeared at the B and B. 'Get whatever you've got together,' he said, 'and we'll be off.'

As we drove west towards Plymouth he tried to put us at our ease. 'Are you OK? Are you all right?' he'd keep turning round to ask. At the same time he was pretty obviously keyed up about the security aspect, making sure we weren't being followed, keeping his eyes skinned for Asian faces, and so on.

We stopped at a little seaside town called Paignton. 'Come on,' Dennis said, 'we'll get you a hot meal.' He checked out this greasy spoon on the seafront for us, then took us in and bought us lunch. Zena had a big plate of fish and chips. I had chips and one of those horrible meat and potato pies they have in such places. It was lovely, the first proper meal we'd had for a long time.

It turned out that Dennis hadn't been in touch with this other daughter of his for fifteen years. Why, we didn't know and didn't want to know. But the last thing he wanted, I reckoned, was to have us two ragamuffins along with him. 'Just drop us off at a pub, Dennis,' I said, 'you need to do this on your own.' We saw this big place on the outskirts of Plymouth called the Hare and Hounds. He checked out the bars for Asian faces and left us there.

After he'd seen his daughter he seemed calmer. As we headed north on the motorway he continued asking whether we were OK. Then he began on more in-depth questions. Not that he made us uncomfortable by probing. He was just clearly deeply curious about our whole situation. He seemed totally incensed that such a thing could happen in the UK in the 1990s. Every now and then you could see this anger of his rising inside him. It was almost as if he was trying to calm himself down, because he'd drive the next twenty miles or so in silence. I got the feeling he didn't want to distress us.

'So, Zena,' he asked at one point, 'what d'you think about your family after all this has happened?'

'I still feel for them,' she replied. 'They're still my flesh and blood. I still love them, even though I know what they're doing is wrong . . .'

When she'd finished it was almost as if he was unable to deal with the honesty of what she'd said. Perhaps he'd been expecting a torrent of hatred. 'Oh, right,' he said. 'Just asking.' He left it at that.

By the time we got to Lincoln it was dark. From the motorway, you could see the floodlit cathedral from miles away, growing larger and larger with each mile that passed. Although we'd only been there three nights, and it hadn't exactly been a relaxing time, I felt strangely relieved to be back. It wasn't home, but at least it was somewhere we knew.

Dennis stopped at an Indian restaurant and picked us all up a takeaway curry. It was a nice thought. He was trying to make Zena feel comfortable. Again, he was very sensitive to the security aspect. He parked twenty yards up the road and went in himself while Zena crouched down on the back seat.

Dennis's bungalow was in a *Brookside*-style cul-de-sac on the edge of the city. It was a pleasant open-plan sort of place with a kitchen and living room all in one. Dennis showed us to one of the bedrooms at the front. Then we heard him tapping on his younger daughter's door down the corridor. 'I've just got some guests with me,' he was saying, 'and they're going to be staying with us for a couple of days, OK?' She must have been asleep because the only response was this muffled groaning sort of noise.

What we didn't know as we sat there gratefully mopping up the rogan josh was that Dennis had just recently gone through a very messy divorce. His ex-wife was extremely hostile to him, and this nineteen-year-old daughter of his was really very unhappy about the whole situation. The next morning her attitude towards us was unbelievable. She barely grunted when we were introduced. Then she was slamming the door whenever she left the room, just generally making it very clear that we weren't welcome. We weren't saying much, just sitting tight on the sofa and trying to be as polite as we could.

On our second day I took Dennis aside in the kitchen. 'Look,' I said, 'I think it's going to be best for all concerned if we just find ourselves a B and B. I really can't see this working out.'

'No, no,' he replied. 'Bear with it.' He was working on a permanent move for us. To Bristol. He was talking to some contacts of his who had a flat down there.

'What kind of contacts?' I asked.

'All you need to know at the moment is they're from a mixed-race marriage.'

'What d'you mean, a mixed-race marriage?' Zena cut in.

'He's Asian and she's white.' He must have seen the appalled look on Zena's face because he added, 'No, no, they're really nice people.'

'They might be nice people,' Zena said, 'but you don't understand. If he's Asian he's going to look upon it as if I was his daughter.'

Dennis took her point but insisted that they weren't the sort of people who'd ever dream of getting in touch with the Asian network. They were close friends of his, liberal professionals, one worked in television.

'In no way is this guy anything approaching a fundamentalist,' he told us. He really wanted to see how far he could

172

get with this plan. It could be very good for us, a completely fresh start in a new place.

'Think it over,' he said.

We didn't want to seem ungrateful to someone who was so obviously doing all he could to help. Maybe, we decided on consideration, it was the right thing. We were so desperate just to get settled somewhere.

'Don't you think,' I said to Dennis the next day, 'that we should get in touch with the police again?' I thought it would be wise at least to call Alan Jones, let him know we were back on his patch.

Dennis thought not. He didn't want to risk them trying to move us on again, he said. He wanted to sort something out for us before they were notified. What he wanted to do was get in touch with the Victim Support lady we'd seen on our previous trip to Lincoln.

So Margaret Jackson reappeared in our lives, through the archway that led into Dennis Baird's kitchen, still in her long tweed skirt and smart waistcoat combination.

The first thing that happened was that Julie, Dennis's sulky daughter, took one look at Margaret and decided she didn't like her. She stormed out of the kitchen. I would have laughed except that as she left she slammed this tumbler she had in her hand down on the melamine surface right by my ear, so hard that it was a miracle it didn't break. I could have throttled her. She must have seen that none of us was a threat to her precious territory. We weren't saying, 'We want to stop here for ever.' We were desperate to get out of that bungalow as fast as we could.

When she'd gone we had a polite little chat with Margaret about what had happened since we'd last met. Zena and I had already decided not to bring up the desperate phone call she'd made from Bournemouth. So we explained, as best we could, what had happened on the Isle of Wight, making sure, again, that we didn't attach any blame to Brenda Steele, even when we came to the point about us having to leave because we'd been married in our real names. Brenda was Margaret's contact and the last thing we wanted to do was upset her. So we just let it ride. Again it was a case of the 'standing on your head syndrome'. We were in trouble. These people were trying to help us. We didn't want to rock the boat.

Luckily for us, Dennis and Margaret seemed to hit it off straight away. They were in complete agreement on the arrangements for our next move. Dennis explained about this possible flat in Bristol and how he was hoping to set up contacts in the police and Housing department and DSS for us down there. Margaret thought it was an excellent plan.

Four evenings later he came through the front door with a long face. 'Bristol's off,' he said.

'What d'you mean?' Zena and I had become quite excited about this move. But Dennis had had a row with one of his DSS contacts. 'Basically,' he said, 'they won't allow you in the city unless you're prepared to give them your real names, NI numbers and dates of birth.' Although we were now officially National Sensitive, we didn't want to go back under our real names. There'd still be the problem with medical cards; we'd still, we felt, be too easily traceable. Once bitten, twice shy.

Dennis was furious. He'd explained everything to the Bristol DSS department but they wouldn't budge. He'd even enlisted Alan Jones's help, but to no avail. ('It was the Bristol police,' he told me later. 'They just didn't want you on their patch.')

'So what do we do now?'

'Don't worry,' Dennis replied. He had an alternative plan. He had this fireman friend, Jeff, who had an empty house available right there in Lincoln. As soon as he'd fixed it up, we could move in.

Meanwhile I'd been in touch with my sister Jenny. It was the first time I'd spoken to any of my family since we'd been on the Isle of Wight, over a month before. It was because we'd been so low, I suppose, that I hadn't felt like calling them. There was no good news to report. Nor were they, any of them, in a position to help us out – financially or in any other practical way. We'd caused them enough grief as it was, we reckoned, without troubling them further.

Mum, Jenny said, was still very unwell. She'd made the move from the old house into a new flat but she was still incredibly upset about the whole situation and really wanted to see me.

When I mentioned this to Dennis he immediately offered to drive us up there. We made a plan to go one evening, just for an hour or so, arriving and leaving in the dark. So I phoned Ryan and arranged to meet him and Mum at the bus station in this little village called Hetherton, up on the moor ten or fifteen miles outside our city. It was the easiest place for us to get to where there would almost certainly be no Asians.

On the way up the motorway Zena told Dennis that he should be very careful to stay away from a particular suburb on the outskirts of the city because her uncle Sulman had a pizza restaurant there.

'Oh, don't worry,' Dennis laughed, 'we won't go anywhere near that.' It was on the opposite side of the city from this village. But as it happened we got totally lost, and Dennis decided to take a tiny country lane which would lead, he thought, across to the main road up on to the moor. Next thing we knew he'd pulled up at a red traffic light and Zena, lying as she was on the back seat, was looking up out of the window straight at a neon sign saying SULMAN'S PIZZAS.

'That's his bloody restaurant!' she shouted.

'What?'

'That's the restaurant my uncle owns.'

'Drive, Dennis!' I yelled at him. 'Drive!'

'Which way, which way?'

'Go right! Go right!'

There'd only been a young lad serving a customer up at

the window. But still, of all the myriad junctions on the edge of our home city, we'd managed to end up there.

Finally we found this remote village of Hetherton, a bundle of lights buried in the dark moor. And there at the bus station was my mother, and my brother Ryan and his wife Linda. The car pulled up and I ran over and hugged them, with the longest squeeze for my frail old mum. And then Zena came over and they all embraced her too. They didn't say anything to our faces but I could tell from the way they were reacting that they were shocked at the look of us. Later, on the phone, Ryan brought it up. 'Eh, Jack,' he said, 'the weight that you've lost – both of you.'

'We've only got an hour or two,' I said. 'Let's get ourselves somewhere we can have a talk.' We drove to a nearby pub and sat in this little private snug area at the back. We had a real catch-up session. Mum took us through the episode of Zena's brothers breaking into her house, and her move. Ryan explained about all the other threats and harassment they'd been getting. We took them through our side of the story.

'Anyway,' I said, finally, 'the good news from our side is we're getting sorted out at last.'

'Don't worry,' Dennis Baird reassured Mum, 'I' taking good care of them, they're in professional hands. Everything's going to be OK.'

It was a very special time for us and an emotional farewell, not knowing when we'd see each other again. Back in the car none of us said anything all the way back down to Lincoln.

Then there was a new and completely unexpected development. Margaret Jackson had been calling by the bungalow to see how we were on quite a number of occasions. Then staying on for a drink and a chat with Dennis.

One evening when I was in the Pig and Whistle with Dennis, we were talking about this and that, our future plans and so on, and he suddenly said, 'She's a really nice woman, isn't she – Margaret?' As soon as he came up with that I thought, 'Oh no, here we go.' She'd already told him she was going through a divorce. Now he wanted to know if I thought she might be interested in him.

'Well,' I said, 'there's only one way you're going to discover, Dennis, isn't there, and that's by asking her out.'

'Oh no. I'm not that kind of guy. I'm quite shy really.'

'Well, you'll never know if you don't ask her,' I said. I was being flippant, but the next thing we knew was they were going off on a date together.

Well, we thought, fair enough, this isn't any business of ours. This is their private life. But then it emerged that their relationship was starting to affect our case. Margaret had apparently said to Dennis, 'You're getting in too deep with these people, you're becoming emotionally involved.'

She could talk. Anyway, having told me about this exchange, Dennis then reassured me. 'Don't worry,' he said. 'I've no intention of dropping you. I've brought you up here and I'm going to do my very best to try to get this whole thing sorted out.'

ZENA:

Margaret Jackson's relationship with her husband was at a very messy stage. She used to come round and moan to Dennis about it all, and Dennis used to moan to her about his problems with his ex-wife and his grumpy daughter Julie, and that's how it all started.

It was interesting because, as they got keener on each other, details of Margaret's private life with her husband used to really wind Dennis up. Her husband wouldn't let her do this, she was supposed to do that, she was meant to cook this particular meal he liked, and so on. It clearly riled Dennis that any man could dominate a woman in that way, especially this woman that he was starting to have these strong feelings for.

By this time, of course, both Jack and I were just

desperate to get out of Dennis's place. As well as this bur-
geoning love affair, we were still getting all the hassle from
Julie, although most of her aggression, it's true, was now
directed towards Margaret. In addition, I seemed to have
taken on the role of permanent unofficial babysitter to
Dennis's two little boys, who lived with his ex-wife but
who came down to his house most afternoons. I didn't
mind helping Dennis in the least but at times I felt as if I
was working for Julie, too. She'd say she'd be back by a
certain hour to look after these lads and then she wouldn't
turn up, so I'd have to cook their supper and put them to
bed. If I'd been my normal self this would all have been
fine, but in the exhausted, run-down state we were in then,
it seemed more than I could cope with.

Julie had a way of making us feel totally unwanted. I
used to try to keep the lowest possible profile, so as not
to annoy her. I took showers rather than baths, kept the
heating off even when it was cool in the evening, so as not
to be running up Dennis's gas bill. Although he'd said we
could use his washing machine, we made an effort not to
have too many changes of clothing, so as not to overdo it.
I'd put the clothes on the circular washing line outside,
rather than use the tumble dryer. And so on.

Yet Julie'd still manage to make me feel we were
imposing horribly.

The other thing that was really making me worried was
that Dennis was totally indiscreet; he didn't seem able to
stop telling people our story. He'd told his ex-wife, and
his ex-wife's boyfriend, and this fireman, Jeff, and other
people in the Pig and Whistle, who'd presumably told other
people, so that you got the feeling that almost everybody
in and around his little cul-de-sac knew what I regarded
as our private and personal circumstances.

Fortunately this fireman Jeff's house, number 3 Albert
Terrace, was now ready. It was a sweet little place, not far
from the centre of town, but in a very secluded street of
redbrick houses tucked away behind a canal. When we'd

178

first seen it, it had been in quite a state, filthy dirty and full of junk. Now, though, Jeff had tidied it up, laid down new carpets, put in a second-hand suite, and made it clean and comfortable. We were thrilled. The main thing was that we had our privacy, which we'd yearned for for so long.

Dennis Baird had got in touch with PC Alan Jones, who'd been so kind and helpful to us the first time we'd been in Lincoln. Now he came down to see us and it was arranged that a panic alarm should be installed by our beds to link us straight through to the police station. Dennis himself paid for a phone to be installed.

This is more like it, we thought.

When we walked in through that door the first thing Jack did, as always, was go upstairs and check the bedroom and bathroom windows; to see how far we'd have to jump if we were ever caught up with. And once we'd moved in we kept to our nightly routine of pushing a sofa against the door of our bedroom last thing after we'd locked up. We no longer slept with the lights on; that was too expensive now we were paying the bills. Nor were we fully dressed; but we still kept T-shirts and underwear on, just in case. Our bags remained packed as always – ready for us to grab if we had to make a dash for it.

14

JACK:
It was the end of May and at last we had a place we could
call our own. It was nicely furnished with a suite and a
TV. Margaret had got together with Alan and his wife to
sort us out with some basic kitchen equipment, an iron
and a kettle.

Once they'd got us settled in, Dennis and Margaret
started making enquiries to see what could be done for us
on a more permanent basis. They told us that they were
looking into trying to sort out a complete, official, identity
change 'package' for us, of the kind that is normally only
given to supergrasses and some special categories of
released long-term prisoner.

They were making contact, they said, with a senior police
officer within the Lincolnshire force, a DCI. He would
write to the Chief Constable of Lincolnshire who would
formally apply on our behalf for this identity change from
Scotland Yard. The package would contain new passports,
NI numbers, medical cards and dates of birth, as well as
work histories, checkable references and previous
addresses, so that we could go out and look for work
without jeopardizing our safety.

Margaret warned us that it might take some time. Six
to nine weeks before a decision would come back from
Scotland Yard about whether or not this could happen. If
it was a 'yes' we'd then have to wait longer for documents
to be sorted out.

But we didn't mind waiting a few weeks. We were
thrilled. We saw this as a final solution to all our problems.

With totally new identities we could start to earn money, our own living, a new life would start.

ZENA:
By this time, Dennis and Margaret were pretty besotted with each other. When they came down to see us, they'd sit together on our sofa and kiss and cuddle like two lovestruck teenagers. I'd think, For heaven's sake stop messing about and get on with it.

We'd sit there of an evening and listen to Margaret's problems about her divorce and Dennis's problems with Julie (who was still very hostile to Margaret) and his ex-wife, and so on. And they were supposed to be counselling us!

Finally Margaret started to fall asleep on us. It's true that she worked full time for the Crown Prosecution Service as well as Victim Support, quite apart from all these extra hassles of her personal life. But she used to arrive to see us so exhausted that after a while she'd just nod off on Dennis's shoulder.

While we waited for this new identity package we were signed on and settled into a routine that involved killing as much time as we could and spending as little money as we could.

We continued to eat our sandwiches and pot noodles, though now, by careful budgeting, we usually had enough money for a proper evening meal as well, from Morrison's, the cut-price place. At the start of each week we'd get a 4 lb bag of oven chips for £1.29 and build our meals round that. So we'd have a tin of stewed steak with chips. Or a tin of spaghetti bolognese with chips. One tin would do the two of us.

Or we'd get four of those cheap frozen beefburgers for 85p – that would do us for a couple of meals. Sometimes I'd make a lentil dhal; you'd get a bag of lentils for 79p and I could get nine curries out of that. Morrison's also did a bag of chapati flour for 79p, so I'd make chapatis and stretch it out further.

We had other ways of economizing too that Jack remembered from his childhood. If we made coffee or tea, for example, we'd just make the one cup and share it, passing it back and forwards between us (a habit we've kept up to this day).

JACK:
I spent more money than I should on cigarettes and Zena and I would often argue about this. So I'd ration myself to five a day. Then I'd make roll-ups with old tabs. Three old fags would make a decent enough smoke.

It goes without saying that there was almost no money left over for drink. Occasionally, if Dennis or Alan came down, I'd go out with them for a pint. But weeks would go by when I'd be on the wagon.

We'd go out for a walk each afternoon, and in the morning Zena liked to throw any stale bread or chapatis out to the ducks on the canal, but most of our time was spent indoors, watching TV. We felt safer there, and I was happier if Zena was outside alone as little as possible. It was very monotonous. We got to the point where we'd get up each morning and circle the programmes we were going to watch in the *TV Quick*. The daytime programmes. That's how bored we were. It was a fairly relentless diet of *Kilroy*, *Oprah*, *Neighbours*, *Home and Away*, *Countdown*, interspersed with news, news and more news. I was probably one of the best-informed people in the country on current affairs. You'd spot the same reports coming round and round, with slightly different intros maybe between lunchtime and ten o'clock.

We didn't obviously have the money for books or magazines and we couldn't sign up at the public library because we had no positive IDs. So it was mainly TV. Sometimes if I heard about a book I wanted to read I might go and look at it in the shop, read it standing up by the shelves, a chapter or so a day. We read all the hostages' books like that. Brian Keenan's, Terry Waite's, John McCarthy and Jill Morrell's. Obviously what they'd gone through was in a completely different league, but I found the way they'd survived their long ordeals fascinating, as well as inspiring.

I wish I could say that, having sacrificed so much for each other, our day-to-day relationship was one of total harmony. But life isn't like that. Of course I still loved Zena as much as ever, but the monotony of being together twenty-four hours a day got to us. We'd have silly squabbles about who was going to put the shopping away, or who was going to make the next pot of tea.

'You make it.'

'Why should I? I made the last one.'

'Bloody hell, does that mean anything? Can't you just get up and make it?'

Then there'd be a deathly silence for about ten minutes while we both sulked and nobody made the tea. But we'd end up talking to each other, obviously, because there was nobody else to talk to.

Every time we argued I used to think to myself, We mustn't do this, we mustn't turn on each other, because this is what they're praying for. Her family. I'm not going to let it happen, because if I do they've won.

ZENA:

Sometimes Jack would go off into these big rants about our situation. Generally it would start with something on the telly. There'd be a programme about Asian culture, or arranged marriages, or whatever. Somebody would be up there on screen saying, 'It's all exaggerated. In Asian communities in Britain we give the freedom to our daughters.' And then all of a sudden Jack would have brought this round to our situation. 'Well, it doesn't effing happen like this in our city,' he'd go.

'No, love. He's not talking about our city, he's talking about down south . . .'

'Well, how can he generalize about arranged marriages like that? It's all bullshit. If people believe that, no wonder they don't take us seriously half the time . . .'

I'd hear his voice going up and up as he got angrier and angrier. He'd go red in the face and I'd think, Any minute now he's going to explode.

So we wouldn't talk to each other for a while. We would sit there and sulk, and one of us would say, 'Go and stand in the corner and sulk. Go on, get in the corner.' Then we'd start to laugh, which would break the stalemate.

Other times when we were cross with each other we'd talk about fields. I'd say, 'I'm not coming into your field, Jack. I know you've left the gate open, you want me in your field to argue. I'm not coming. We'll just close the gate and stay away from each other for a while.'

He used to call me Kashmir's answer to Vera Duckworth; in return I told him he was getting more like Victor Meldrew every day.

JACK:
When things were going better we'd sit there together and spin up little fantasies. We'd talk about what kind of house we'd have, if we ever got finally settled safely somewhere. We'd go into tremendous detail: the design of the wallpaper, the curtains, what kind of lounge suite we'd have. Would it be covered in cloth, or leather? What sort of carpet would we have? Would we *have* a carpet, or just bare varnished boards? Or seagrass, or cork tiles?

We'd move upstairs to the bedrooms and bathrooms. How many would there be? The master bedroom would have an *en suite*, of course, but would it be carpeted? What colour would the bath and basins be? Would we have a wooden toilet seat or a plastic one? Would the bed be pine or antique? Would there be a chest of drawers, a tallboy, or fitted cupboards?

Then I'd be out in the garden, working out what kind of lawn I'd want. What kind of flowers I'd plant. The trees that came with the garden. There'd be a blossoming cherry here, as there'd been at the bottom of Dennis Baird's garden. There'd be shrubs there, and geraniums in pots there. Would there be an ornamental pond? And if so, would it have goldfish, or carp?

It was as if we'd put virtual reality helmets on. We'd be there, sitting under the apple tree with a beer, having just mown the lawn with one of those buggies you see advertised on the TV all the time in the summer. It was quite a contrast to the bit of backyard we did have, which was totally overgrown with a sort of trailing ivy with tiny yellow flowers. As the summer progressed this ivy became infested with wasps. There must have been a couple of nests in there because some days you'd go out and there was just this huge cloud of wasps. I borrowed some shears from Alan and had a real go at this ivy, clipping it back to the bare stems. But it didn't get rid of the wasps. By August it got to the point where Zena used to take the laundry out to the line with a towel wrapped round her head.

Sometimes these fantasies of ours would take us abroad for a holiday. We're settled now, with decent jobs and a nice home – so where would we take off on holiday? I wanted to see America. New York, of course. Chicago. LA. San Francisco. Then I wanted to go to Montana, Ohio, that kind of cowboy country.

Zena was keener on Europe. She wanted to see the art and the galleries. She'd seen a programme on the TV about the field where Van Gogh had shot himself and she wanted to visit that. She wanted to see his paintings in the museum in Amsterdam. She wanted to see Monet's house in France and the garden he'd painted. Then she wanted to go to Italy and see the ceiling of the Sistine Chapel.

So how would we get there? On a plane or through the tunnel? How much money would we need for a week? Would we fly from this airport or that airport? Which hotel would we stay in? Would we learn enough of the language to get by? Or would we need a guide or a translator? What clothes would we take?

We'd go off into great detail about this, planning our luggage and clothes and other bits and bats. Zena would want a lot of luggage, of course. I'd tease her about that. I could see her like something out of one of the old films, going through Customs with three porters and a huge pile of baggage. Eight matching suitcases, six vanity cases, hatboxes, the works. I'd be happy with a rucksack and a holdall. A few pairs of jeans, a few T-shirts, socks, maybe one suit at the bottom in case we did go somewhere posh, a shirt, a tie, a pair of trainers, a pair of walking boots, shorts – and that's me done.

'So how are you going to fit all that into one holdall?' she'd say. So I'd explain how, if you fold up jeans this way, you can get them in. And so on.

We'd all but be there. We could hear the bustle of the airport, the whine of the jets, feel the excitement of getting on the plane and taking off. We'd see the landscape of clouds below you and the blue sky above. The taxi at the other end. The hotel room.

ZENA:
Another thing we used to do to pass the time was Spot the Ball. We'd go down to the newsagent and pick up a load of Spot the Ball forms which we'd take home and fill in. We used to sit there for hours drawing these fine lines on these sheets and working out where the ball was in these competitions. We couldn't afford to send them in, of course.

Occasionally, if we had 50p spare, we might actually post one off. One Monday morning when I came down there was a slip under the doormat addressed to me. *Congratulations*, it said. *You have won* SPOT THE BALL.

'Look, honey,' I said, running back upstairs, 'we've won!'

We opened it up and guess what we'd won? Three hundred and fifty extra Spot the Ball crosses. I was gutted.

During the flat season we'd follow the racing on Channel Four. We'd sit there together and pretend we had money. Jack taught me about odds and picking favourites and everything, so we'd bet on each race. We'd start the afternoon with £500 cash and keep a tally of how much we'd made.

Sometimes one of us would accumulate thousands while the other would be totally broke. Jack used to be furious with the way I quite often picked winners, because I just chose the names I liked the sound of, or the best-looking jockey, or whatever.

By the end of the afternoon, when I was a rich woman, he'd be going, 'Love, lend us £100.' So if he behaved himself I might oblige.

At other times we used to talk about writing a book. About what had happened to us. I didn't actually think our story would make a book. I thought everyone had bad times and this was just something you had to get through. But Jack was sure it would, especially when we watched the true-life stories on TV. '*They* think they've had it hard,' he'd say. 'They should hear our story.'

'What would you call it, if it ever did come to it?' I asked.

Run Long, Run Hard was the title he liked most. But then he decided that sounded too much like a sports book.

We were pretty near the centre of Lincoln and when Jack went up to sign on I might walk round the shops for half an hour looking at the windows, fantasizing, again, about the outfits I'd buy if I ever had the money. In the department stores I'd take advantage of anything that was free, like the perfume testers; I'd spray myself with a couple of those. Then I'd go into Topshop and try things on in the changing booths. Just to see what the new fashions looked like. I could never buy them but it made me feel better to try them on.

I'd have a look at the new nail varnishes and lipsticks and handcreams and remember the days when I was in a position to afford them. How I'd taken all that for granted! Back home I used to do a full French manicure probably every other day. My hands were in perfect condition. I had twenty or thirty different nail varnishes.

Jack always set a time for me to be back, though. It was OK for me to be out, but he'd be worried sick if I didn't get back when we'd agreed.

I used to be very fond of drawing at home, too. I found a shop in Lincoln where everything they sold cost 50p. I bought this fat pad of cheap drawing paper. Since I obviously couldn't justify spending money on coloured pens or paints I made do with a 2B pencil. That kept me amused for hours, sketching away. I did drawings for Jack, and then PC Jones's little boy.

Because we were virtually housebound I started on an exercise routine. I didn't want to get to a stage where my body completely gave in on me, so I made out a little chart. I wrote on it: *Zena Chadhaury – these are exercises I'll do, every day.* Underneath I had little boxes to fill in, to keep me up to the mark. They were just basic things to keep me in shape: press-ups, star jumps, sit-ups. But they did make me feel better. Jack tried for a while, too, but he didn't keep at it long.

Week after week came and went and there was still no firm news about this package. Gradually Dennis and Margaret stopped visiting us. We couldn't get hold of them on the phone and our messages went unanswered.

Eventually, Jack got through to Dennis. 'Have you had any news about our package?' he asked.

'You'll have to talk to Margaret about that,' Dennis replied.

'I thought you were both doing it.'

'She's taken over.'

'Could you ask her to call us back, then? She's not been returning our calls.'

Nothing happened for three days. We just sat in that little front room waiting for the phone to ring.

'Right,' I said on day four, 'this is ridiculous. I'm getting on that bloody phone.' I called Margaret and got straight through.

'I'm sorry, Zena,' she said, 'we're off to Scotland for a short holiday. We'll have to sort it all out when we get back.'

'No,' I replied, 'that's not good enough.' We'd been sitting there waiting for this package every day for nine weeks by then. 'We need to know what's going on. If you tell us who the DCI is who's written the letter for us then I can get on to him direct.'

'I'm sorry, I can't tell you that.'

'I need to know his name,' I insisted. 'We're going to go down to the police station and find out what's happened to this letter.'

'Oh, I really wouldn't advise you to do that. That could be counter-productive.'

Counter-productive! I badgered on at her until eventually I managed to get a name out of her. It was a DCI Fisher.

JACK:
So I rang up Lincolnshire Headquarters and got through to DCI Fisher. He was fine about seeing us. 'Right,' he said, 'if you want to see me, come down next week one afternoon.'

He was a pretty experienced-looking officer, in his fifties, I should guess, definitely towards the end of his career. He certainly gave the impression that he knew what he was up to.

'Right,' he said, when we'd got settled opposite him in his office, 'so what can I do for you?'

'Well obviously,' I began, 'you know Margaret Jackson and Dennis Baird are arranging for us to have an identity change . . .'

He looked across the desk at us with bemusement. 'I've heard of Margaret Jackson,' he said, 'but who's Dennis Baird?'

He'd never even *heard* of him. 'I think we'd better start from the beginning here,' I said. So we went through our story all over again. Eventually we got to the part about the package.

'I believe,' I said, 'that some weeks ago a letter was written to the Chief Constable, which was then to be sent down to Scotland Yard for their approval . . .'

'A letter?' he said. 'Oh yes, I do remember something about a letter, but where it is at this stage I'm not exactly sure. I'll have to look into it . . .'

I was dumbfounded. In our meetings with Dennis and Margaret we'd been led to believe that this letter was on the desk of someone in Scotland Yard. Now we discovered it hadn't even reached the Chief Constable in Lincoln. So we came out of this DCI Fisher's office and walked back up Lincoln High Street like a pair of deranged nutters.

'Right,' I said, 'I'm going to get on that bloody phone and find out exactly what Dennis and Margaret have been up to all this time.'

I rang and got their answerphones. I rang and got their secretaries. I left messages, but they were still, we could only assume, away. There was nothing coming back. Eventually I managed to make contact with Margaret Jackson.

'Margaret,' I said, 'we've been down to see DCI Fisher and he's never even *heard* of Dennis, wasn't sure where the letter was, apparently it hasn't even been sent . . .'

Before I could finish she was screaming down the phone at me – and I'll never forget this – '*I know what your game is!*' Then she hung up. I put down the phone in total amazement.

'What did she say? What did she say?' Zena was asking.

'She screamed, "I know what your game is!" and hung up.'

I just couldn't work it out. What the bloody hell was she talking about?

ZENA:

We'd been so grateful for the help they'd given us, and now, it seemed, they didn't want to listen to us or have anything to do with us any more. It felt as if they'd just wiped their feet on us, like a doormat, and walked away.

I got really wound up about it. Dennis Baird had been so full of ideas and promises, but then nothing ever actually happened. Everything just seemed to fade and die away.

Months had passed, and we were getting so frustrated. You could feel this anger building up inside you. Stuck for ever inside the four walls of that little front room there was nowhere for it to go. I got to the point where I wanted to smash things, kick walls, throw stuff around, scream; just to stop myself from doing damage to myself or anyone else.

Sometimes the only way I could let go was by crying, which I would do for hours and hours, face down on the bed upstairs.

All that long summer and autumn we kept coming down with illnesses. They were all basically related to stress, I think. But we hadn't got any proper medical advice because we still didn't think we could risk getting our medical cards from our home city. When I went down with an agonizing bout of stomach cramps Margaret Jackson had arranged for me to see a doctor, but he'd made it very clear that he couldn't see us again without our records. If he saw people not on his list, he told us, he risked being struck off. So the prescription had to be put in Margaret's name, and after that we just had to make do with medicines we could get from the chemist's.

JACK:

Because my mother was so ill I was still in contact with my sister Jenny. She told me that Zena's family had seemed to be keeping a low profile. I'd been worried about this. 'It's quiet,' I said to Zena, 'I don't like it.'

Now, though, my brother-in-law Dan told me, the brothers had started frequenting pubs in my old area offering a reward for information about me. Dan had been out one night and one of the thousand and one acquaintances I've got in those places had come up and told him that he'd been approached by Kasim wanting to know if he knew where I was.

'Listen,' he'd said when he'd drawn a blank, 'if you do hear owt, there's a reward out for 'em. There's serious money up if anyone knows anything about where they are.'

On his way home Dan had run into Miriam on the corner of the street. God knows what had sparked it off – whether she'd given Dan a dirty look or whatever – but Dan was a walking time bomb.

'Tell your brothers,' he said to her, 'not to approach my friends offering money for information about Jack. If I hear any more of this they'll have me to answer to. OK?'

A week or so after this incident Jenny started getting anonymous phone calls. She didn't recognize any of the voices, but she heard this Asian music in the background. She reckoned the calls were coming from an Asian restaurant.

They said things like they were going to come round and petrol-bomb the house while her kids were at home. Then they started threatening to kidnap one of the kids and 'chop them up'. These calls were happening two or three times a night and Jenny was obviously incredibly distressed about them. Dan, too. He was ranting and raving on the phone to me about it. I used to get so incensed that I couldn't do anything about it. I couldn't even protect my own sister. Jenny went to the police and got her phone tapped. The calls stopped. But she and Dan still decided to take their kids out of the local school and go to their housing federation to apply for a move. They wanted to leave the area completely. They'd had enough harassment.

It boiled me up inside that they'd been effectively forced to do this. That Adie and Scott had had to leave school and friends and start over again in a new area. Who the fuck did these people think they were?

I didn't marry a culture or a tradition, I married an individual, a woman. I could understand the family, to a certain extent, having this great concern that their sister had run off with this bloke who was X amount of years older and who had not exactly had the straightest past. I could even understand their frustration. That they were unable to track us down, have their way. But what I could not understand was how they thought what they were doing was right.

They didn't seem to care that they were completely ignoring the law of the land they were in. As far as they were concerned it was as if I had stolen a piece of their property.

I felt a terrible anger and hate that they could inflict this not only on their own daughter, and on me, but on my mother and my sisters. Because that's one thing I noticed about them. They never made any direct threats to Ryan or Dan – it was always aimed at the women, who were the easier targets.

The other thing that made me furious about the brothers was that I knew only too well how they had behaved. When I'd been friends with them I'd been a party to their nights out. And here they were suddenly throwing this cloak of Islam around themselves and saying, 'This is terrible, this can't go on.' I thought, You two-faced hypocritical bastards. What right have you to stand up on your high horse and say what we're doing is wrong?

Though I felt all this, I never directed any of it at Zena. I think one of the reasons our relationship is so strong is that we've always sat down and talked these feelings through. God knows we've had plenty of time to do it. Zena has always said to me, 'I can understand your anger.' And I've never come off the phone – even after hearing about my mother or my sister, or the threats to the children – and taken it out directly on her. Blamed her or screamed at her, 'Your fucking family!'

ZENA:
At that time Jenny knew we were in Lincoln. We'd had to give her our number because of Jack's mother being so ill.

The anonymous calls to her were from either my brothers or from Salim, or friends of theirs. When it got to the point that they were actively threatening Jenny's two little boys I could have understood if she'd just turned round and said, 'Your bloody sister's in Lincoln, OK? Now leave me and my family alone!'

I had such a huge respect for her that she kept silent, even when she had to take them out of school and move house. Privately I thought, I may have lost one family but I've gained another.

Jack used to rage about the hypocrisy of my brothers and he was right. This campaign they were waging against us had nothing, as far as I was concerned, to do with the religion I believed in. It was all to do with pride and loss of face. They were using the religion to justify what they were doing. But I hadn't done anything wrong. I'd fallen in love with a man I wanted to spend the rest of my life with. The Holy Quran says that you are supposed to accept the man you marry. So where was the sin?

15

JACK:
PC Alan Jones was a totally genuine bloke. 'I'm just a foot soldier,' he'd said to me once. 'I don't have the rank to action what needs to be done, but I'll do what I can.' He used to come down to see us sometimes in his off-duty hours. He sympathized with us and listened and encouraged – none of which he had to do.

He was married and he told me more than once that he and his wife really admired our persistence and commitment to each other. 'It's hard to believe how you've stuck together through all this,' he said.

He and his wife had been going through a rough patch themselves and had sorted out their differences because of us, he said. We had put their problems in perspective. In the state we were in – frustrated, depressed, wondering daily what the hell we'd got ourselves into – it was heartwarming to hear this.

One night in the early autumn Alan appeared with a senior police officer we'd not seen before – a DCI Russell. DCI Fisher had retired over the summer and Russell had come down to introduce himself as the man who was taking over our case. I didn't like him from the word go.

Zena had been doing a bit of drawing, and had come up with this big picture of Mickey Mouse for Alan Jones's son. She was in the front room showing Alan this when DCI Russell grabbed hold of my arm and pulled me into a corner.

'Eh,' he said, giving me a bit of a leer. 'Does she know all about you? Does she know your full record?'

You smug bastard, I thought. 'Yeah,' I said, 'she does, as it happens.'

'Just asking,' he replied.

A month or so later Russell turned up with Alan Jones again. They had very good news. Special Branch had approved the package request. It would now go ahead. We needed to choose two new names for our new identities. After a night or two of excited discussion we came up with Frank and Elizabeth Clayton. Zena would use the name Beth.

So we changed from Mike and Sonya to Frank and Beth. At home, to each other, as well as outside to everyone else. Even in our most private moments we used these names, till they became, once again, second nature to us.

Then just before Christmas Margaret Jackson and Dennis Baird reappeared. The package would be with us, they told us, shortly after Christmas. (We were so pleased that it was finally happening that I didn't feel it was appropriate to bring up Margaret's strange behaviour of the summer, slamming the phone down on me and saying 'I know what your game is.')

Now, they said, we needed to choose a place where we'd like to start our new lives. Initially we suggested staying where we were. Our house was comfortable and if we could go out and get work we'd have been more than happy there. But no, they told us, that wouldn't be a good idea.

DCI Russell was adamant that, package or no package, we couldn't stay in Lincoln. The 'safe house' at Albert Terrace was needed for someone else, he said. If we stayed, the police protection we'd been given to date would be removed, panic button and all. So we suggested Skegness, still in the county of Lincoln. That wouldn't do either, they said. Russell's argument was that we could be traced from Lincoln to Skegness too easily. It seemed pretty clear to me that the local force wanted us off their patch. We weren't in any position to argue, so we discussed it and decided eventually that our best option would be to return to the

Isle of Wight. We thought our best shot at getting properly settled would be to use the contacts we'd made down there – Brenda Steele, Susan Bates, Emma Hillier. Despite the strange way they'd treated us they were the only people – apart from this lot in Lincoln – who knew us and could vouch for us, give us the references and perhaps even introductions we'd need to get work. As for the marriage certificate, it had been almost a year since we'd left the island. If Zena's brothers or the private investigator had tracked us through that, they would have been there by now, searched the place from top to toe with a fine toothcomb, and drawn a blank. It would be an effective double-bluff, I reckoned, to return.

So we suggested this, and Margaret, Dennis and Alan tried to put us off there, too. 'I think you want to think of somewhere else,' they kept telling us.

'Why?'

'Because you were married on the island in your real names.'

I explained my theory about the double-bluff, but they didn't buy it. So this argument went backwards and forwards between us without resolution.

Then one eventful night in early February a meeting was called. We huddled round in our little front room in Albert Terrace, and once again began discussing our move. All of a sudden, Dennis Baird looked up from his papers and, with a sigh of impatience, said, 'You know full well why you can't go back to the Isle of Wight.'

'No.'

'Oh, come off it!'

'Hang on a minute,' I said. 'You've come this far now, let's put our cards on the table. What d'you mean?'

He looked from one to the other of us. 'Because,' he said, 'you took the money.'

Zena and I were shell-shocked. We just stared at each other in disbelief. 'You what?' I said. 'What money? What are you saying?'

'When you were on the Isle of Wight,' he said, speaking in this slow, deliberate manner, 'you took money belonging to Emma Hillier, twenty-odd pounds, and you also owe money to the landlady of the B and B where you stayed in Sandown. Your housing benefit wasn't fully paid.'

I exploded. I couldn't believe what he was saying. After all this time it was like a piece of a jigsaw being fitted in. The reason why we'd been told to leave the Isle of Wight, Margaret Jackson's change of attitude when we'd called from Bournemouth, everything.

'So that's the reason,' I said, 'why they married us in our real names, on the island. So that we'd have to go?'

'Yes,' he replied.

Zena had lost it now. 'Right!' she was shouting. 'That's it. I'm ringing up Brenda Steele. I'm not standing for this! No one puts a twenty-pound theft charge on to us and gets away with it.'

'Oh no, Zena,' Margaret was saying. 'I shouldn't do that.'

'I'm going to.'

'You can do anything when you get desperate,' Alan said.

Zena smacked the table with her fist she was so angry. 'You don't know what the word desperate means!' she shouted. 'When you've got to see someone go to bed hungry of a night – that's desperate. When you're tramping the streets, cold and wet, not knowing where the next roof over your head's going to be – that's desperate. Don't you talk to me about desperation—'

'It doesn't matter,' Margaret cut in. 'We didn't believe her anyway.'

'What d'you mean you didn't believe her?' said Zena. 'You've just sat here, after nine months, and brought it up. How d'you think that makes us feel? After all this time, when we've been sitting in your company praising that woman. We haven't had a bad word to say about her despite what she did to us. If you knew this you should have just told us.'

'It doesn't matter,' Margaret repeated. 'Emma didn't report it to the police.'

'But we didn't take it!' Zena insisted.

I looked over at Alan. He was just sitting there with his head down. He had become like a friend to us. Not just a police officer – a friend.

'Did you know this?' I asked.

He looked up at me and said, 'Yeah. But I know,' he went on, 'that you didn't take it. We're all in agreement that you didn't.'

We were both outraged – but in two very different ways. From Zena's point of view it was because she comes from a very high-caste family and it's an insult to be classed as a thief. I, on the other hand, had lived on the wrong side of the law. It wasn't so much that they had turned round and said, 'You're a thief.' I mean, sticks and stones. The outrage with me was because I hadn't taken it. I know I had a past. I don't need other people to point that out. But I have got principles.

We'd been staying in that cottage as Emma's guests. She had left us in charge of her home for the weekend. It was a beautiful house full of beautiful gear – stereo system, VCR, colour TV, you name it. If I had wanted to I could have organized a van, cleared that place out, sold everything on the other end of the island and then pissed off. But it's like the old saying, 'You don't bite the hand that feeds you.' These people were being kind to us and no way would I have helped myself to even a pound coin if I'd found one. As for the bed and breakfast, as we told them now, we still had a receipt from the Sandown lady showing that when she'd received the housing benefit our account was fully settled.

So the Isle of Wight was off. We couldn't obviously go back to a place where we were alienated from all the people who might otherwise have helped us. As for the twenty pounds, it was our word against theirs. And who were the locals going to believe? The people they knew or this known thief who'd just turned up with an Asian woman?

So the discussions went on and they kept bringing up this one particular town. I can't say where it is because we're still hiding there today.

They kept saying to us, If you go to P— we can set you up with a place to live, with funding for the move and basic furnishings, and when the package arrives you'll be sorted. P— is not a place any of your relatives are likely to find you. You can start your new lives. And once again we believed them.

The first thing that went wrong was the 'package'. Dennis and Margaret turned up a few days later with Alan. 'We've got good news,' they said. 'The package has arrived!' There was only one problem – our new identities contained no new dates of birth and no personal histories or references.

While it was obviously a great thing to have got the passports and NI numbers and – in due course – medical cards, without a checkable personal history what use were they? I'd be going for a job interview and I wouldn't be able to mention any qualifications or experiences or references or schools I'd been to. What was I going to say?

'You'll have to invent some,' Alan said.

Had he never tried to get work? Didn't he know that in 99.5 percent of cases employers check references, and if they're found to be false you're out of there before they can say 'clock off'?

'We were just trying to keep your hopes up,' Alan added.

Zena was furious. 'We didn't need to be told a load of crap,' she said to me. 'They should have been straight down the line with us.'

Once again their story was changing from minute to minute. We didn't know what to believe, didn't know whether we were coming or going. But we went along with it. What else could we do? At the start of March, a year and a month after we'd run away, the day finally came for our move to P—.

The money for a deposit on our new property, we were told, had been released, although I wasn't allowed to have it till we'd actually found a place. Then it would be handed over to the landlord. What they thought I was going to do with this money if they gave it to me direct I have no idea. Run off to Barbados on my own, I imagine.

So how were things going to be arranged? I asked. Would somebody take me to P—? Would they give me a travel warrant so I could take the train?

'No,' Alan said, 'you'll have to make your own way there.'

'How do I do that? Can I get funding?'

'You can't.'

So I ended up getting up at six one morning and hitching, with a tenner from Margaret Jackson and another tenner we'd saved from our dole in my pocket. I was lucky with lifts and made reasonable time. I'd already looked up the addresses of a number of local estate agencies in Lincoln library. The game plan was that I should go into one of these places and say, 'Hello, I'm Frank Clayton, I've got X amount of money, do you have any properties available?' Then, once I'd found one that would take me, and got a letter from the agency stating that I did have the property, I should phone back and the money would be released by the DSS. The following day Zena would come down with Alan or Dennis and the agreement would be signed and the money handed over.

So I got to P— and eventually found an agency that was willing to do this. Then I rang back Lincoln and spoke to Margaret Jackson. 'Right,' I said, 'I've found a place that's going to accept this arrangement. I'll start seeing what they've got, shall I?'

'I'm sorry, Mike,' she said, 'you've got to come back to Lincoln because there's been a slight problem.'

'What d'you mean, there's been a slight problem?'

'Somebody's forgotten to have a word with the DSS and notify them that the police are involved.'

'You what? But I'm here now.'

'I'm sorry, Mike, there's nothing more I can do. You'll have to come back.'

So I took the train back to Lincoln, using the money I'd been going to spend on an overnight stop. When I arrived Dennis was waiting for me on the platform. I was absolutely fuming.

'What the hell's going on, Dennis?' I said.

He was genuinely apologetic. The woman who ran the DSS social fund – where this grant was coming from – had refused point-blank to let the money go without authority from the police. And that problem, apparently, couldn't be sorted out on the spot, even though the Lincoln police had known about our situation almost from the beginning.

I walked down the platform shaking my head in disbelief. 'This is turning into a farce, Dennis,' I said.

Back at the house Zena was sitting there surrounded by packed bags. Once again she'd been let down.

Finally the red tape was cut through, the money was made available, and the big day came for us to move. This time we were to be accompanied by the entire team. They arrived first thing in the morning. Dennis with Margaret in his Nissan Micra, Alan following in an unmarked police estate car. We loaded the cars up with our cases and boxes, shut the door on Albert Terrace for, we prayed, the last time, and off we went.

This time the idea was to travel to P—, find a letting agency, organize a place for us to live, then have a meeting with the three crucial contacts that had been made for us: one from Housing, one from Unemployment and one from the DSS.

Needless to say we got lost on the way and arrived late. 'Right,' said Dennis, 'what we'd better do is this. We'll go to the meeting now and we'll get your claim and everything sorted out before we go to an agency, because time's pressing on.' Zena and Margaret would wait for us, mean-while, in a nearby café.

So we went to the DSS and into the meeting. There before me were two guys. One from Unemployment, and one from the DSS. 'Isn't there supposed to be someone else here?' I asked. 'From Housing?' We'd been told that we were going to get top priority on the council list. These two contacts just looked at each other and shrugged – it was news to them.

Then Dennis's mobile phone went. It was Margaret. She'd got bored with waiting in the café and had decided to go shopping. 'You're doing what?' Dennis was saying, pacing up and down to one side of these two bewildered officials. 'We're trying to have a meeting here, love.' A little later she phoned back again. She was hungry, and moving on to McDonald's for lunch.

By the time we'd filled in all the forms it was two o'clock. One of these men looked at his watch and said, 'Well, you know the offices close at half-four, don't you? If you haven't found a place by then you'll have to stay in the DSS B and B.'

I was going mental, because the one place neither Zena nor I wanted to end up was the DSS B and B. That was the ultimate nightmare. The others were going back to Lincoln that evening and then where would we be? Right back to square one, in a new county, with, on our experience to date, absolutely no guarantee that anyone would know our story or be able to help us.

So we sped to McDonald's and picked up the women. Then at last we were heading off round the estate agents. But every single one that we went into refused to touch us. We'd even missed our chance with the one I'd seen two weeks before – that property had gone. The problem was that we had no references, no jobs, there was nothing they could put on paper.

'This is exactly what I said would happen,' I said to Alan. 'The work that we should have put in back in Lincoln hasn't been done and this is the result.' All along our advisers had been telling us that if we had the hard cash to put over the table, the agencies would take us. And I'd been trying to explain that the world just doesn't work like that.

Here I was, walking in with this police officer who was showing his warrant card and saying, 'I can vouch for this person'. Obviously they were going to think, 'Oh yeah? What's going on here? The Old Bill's taking him round and there's the clan sitting outside with the two cars full of luggage, Margaret Jackson and Dennis Baird holding hands like teenage sweethearts in the front. It was like something out of a bloody *Carry On* film.

I was getting desperate by now. 'Look,' I said, 'let's get a local paper, get ourselves based somewhere, and start making some phone calls to private landlords. That is the only way we are going to find a place this afternoon before five o'clock.'

Both Dennis and Alan had mobile phones on them, but Margaret Jackson wouldn't hear of us using them. It was too expensive, she said. So we wasted yet more time hunting for a payphone. In the end we found this little club bar, full of old ladies playing bingo. 'Right,' I said, 'let's park up here and start ringing.'

We walked in and the first thing Alan did was go up to the bar and get everyone a drink. Margaret Jackson went straight over to the fruit machine, which just happened to be right next to the phone. And I got a pile of ten p's and started ringing round, trying to sound convincing against the clanging and whirring and buzzing as our Victim Support counsellor attempted to hit the jackpot.

Eventually I got through to this one lady. 'We're new here in P——,' I told her. 'I'm with my wife's parents, in a car, and we're very keen to get something sorted out today. Could we come over now and have a look at this property you've got advertised?'

'Oh yes, certainly.'

'Right,' I said, putting the phone down, 'I think I've found a place.'

'That's marvellous,' said Margaret Jackson as she slipped her last token into the fruit machine. 'That's great,' said Dennis Baird and Alan Jones as they finished their pints. And off we went to rendezvous with this woman at a nearby garage. Zena, bless her, had agreed to say that she'd lost her parents in a car crash and these were her foster parents. This was part of the history that we'd had to make up.

We followed this lady to the edge of P—, over a railway bridge and sharp left off the road on to a dirt track. At one side was a scrapyard. At the other a sewage plant. The main railway ran alongside. Tucked away in the middle of this was a row of six soot-blackened brick cottages – Waterworks Row. The front half of the unmodernized one at the end – number 6a – was the flat she was letting.

Now if at that stage somebody had come up to us and said, 'How about this beautiful detached cardboard box, only X amount per month,' we'd have taken it. We were now less than half an hour away from being put back into the DSS B and B.

After the deal had been signed, the three of them drove us back up the hill to a nearby parade of shops, half a mile away beyond a big roundabout.

We sat down and Dennis bought us all a drink.

'You are two completely normal people now,' Alan told us. Those bits of paper they'd given us had suddenly transformed us, apparently. We were now Frank and Elizabeth Clayton. The whole of the previous two years had been totally wiped out.

Before we'd left Lincoln we'd had to sign legal documents saying we would never use the names Michael Burnley or Sonya Atkinson again. Now we were told not to talk to anybody about our story or our circumstances. We asked for a contact in Special Branch. We were refused. If we ever did get spotted, or caught up with, or one dark night the front door did get smashed through, we were, they told us, to use 999 like anyone else.

It was quite an emotional farewell. Because I could see, as far as Dennis was concerned, and Alan too, that they knew they'd failed. The system had no way of dealing with our situation. They'd tried to help us, but now, it was clear, they'd given up. They just wanted out. We'd been like a novelty at first. But gradually that novelty had worn off and we'd become a headache. So, once again, we'd been shoved over that county line, to become somebody else's problem.

16

Zena:
The next morning we were woken at eight o'clock sharp by a thundering crash of metal.

'What's that?' I said, sitting bolt upright in bed.

Jack leapt up to investigate. We seriously thought there'd been a train crash or something. But it was only a truck full of scrap aluminium dumping the first load of the day – our new weekday alarm call.

When I got out of bed I was itching all over. The lower half of my legs were covered in little red dots. I couldn't figure out what they were. Jack took one look at them and said, 'Fleas.' He remembered the rash from his childhood.

The night before we'd been so desperate not to end up back in the DSS B and B that we'd just signed on the dotted line. Now we had a chance to look around our new home. It was the front half of one of these six little cottages: a tiny kitchen, bathroom and bedroom upstairs; downstairs a living area about six foot by ten, more like a corridor than a room.

For heating it had a broken fireplace without a flue, which smoked terribly and never provided much warmth. There was a battered door at the front and a window that looked as if it was about to fall off. At the back, beyond a boarded-off door, was the back half – a little bedsit housing another young couple. Behind, a narrow strip of wild garden ran down twenty feet or so to the main railway line, with express trains on the hour every hour.

Normally I'm the first to make the best of things, look

on the bright side, keep going. Now, though, I sank into a terrible depression. I couldn't seem to summon up the energy even to wash, let alone cook or iron or look after Jack. It was mid-March, still freezing cold, even with the fire lit, so I sat wrapped in a coat or a blanket for days on end. I felt alienated, lost, and terribly frightened.

JACK:
Zena had become extremely ill. Not just physically but mentally. She had similar symptoms to those I'd had in Bournemouth. She wouldn't, couldn't, do anything. I was absolutely petrified about the state of her.

One morning I heard her crying and I ran upstairs. 'What's wrong, what's wrong?' I was shouting.

'I can't open the door,' she said.

She was standing there like a lunatic, wrapped in a blanket, shaking so much she couldn't get a grip on the handle.

She began to get the painful stomach cramps again. When she started passing blood with her water I decided it was time to take her to see a doctor. Our new medical cards hadn't arrived yet, but I knew they were being prepared.

The first man we saw was an old fellow, very much from the grin-and-bear-it school of medicine. Despite the fact that Zena had these stomach pains and was now passing blood he didn't bother, even basically, to check her over. He just gave her some suppositories. 'Use these for a week, young lady,' he said breezily, 'and it'll clear up.'

I had this rash of tiny spots all over my face and torso, just under the skin. 'Can you tell me what these are?' I asked.

'Teenage spots, young man.'

'But I'm thirty years old.'

'Well, these things do recur.'

He was basically an old quack.

Zena used the suppositories and the cramps continued. When she had one particularly agonizing bout, and more bleeding, we managed to see a much younger, more switched-on doctor in the same practice – Dr Gill. He examined us thoroughly.

'If I didn't know better,' he said, when he'd finished, 'I'd say you were both suffering from extreme stress.'

We said nothing. We'd been told to say nothing, so we said nothing.

Week after week during that spring and early summer we went back to the surgery, with new things wrong with us every time. Eventually, after a long discussion, we decided we'd break our silence. We made an appointment with Dr Gill and told him everything. He sat there very patiently and listened. At the end he looked us up and down slowly and said, 'I knew it. I just knew there was something more to you two.'

It was partly the sheer number of ailments we'd been coming down with, he said. Also the fact that our medical notes had taken an unusually long time to arrive and when they had arrived had been brand new. Now he gave Zena a full examination and told her she'd need an operation. I was more or less OK, though we agreed it would be a good plan to remove the tattoos on my hands, one of which still said *Jack*.

Having broken our silence with him, and got sorted out properly as a result, we decided, again after a lot of discussion, that we'd try to speak to somebody in the police. We both felt terribly insecure in Waterworks Row. I thought we needed a contact who knew of our full situation and would be there to help us in an emergency.

At the back of the pub in this village-suburb we were living in was an estate of police houses. Over the occasional drink down there I'd got to know a couple of the local officers. Now I decided to approach one of them formally.

'Could I have a private word with you?' I asked Simon Chalker one evening.

'Sure, Frank,' he said. We found a quiet table at the back. 'So what can I do for you, mate?'

'For reasons I can't tell you now,' I said, 'I need to contact someone within the force. It's going to have to be a high-ranking officer. It's in connection with SO11.'

SO11 is the department within the Special Branch that deals with new identities. As soon as PC Chalker heard that, he gulped down his pint and was gone. Truly, if I'd said, 'By the way, I'm gay and I want to make love to you here and now,' I wouldn't have got a quicker reaction. 'I'll be in touch,' he said as he dashed off.

But after a few days he got back in contact with me. He'd arranged a meeting for us with two guys from Special Branch, in a quiet pub by the canal. So we all sat down in this dark corner. Me, Zena, PC Chalker and the two Special Branch officers.

'We shouldn't really be meeting you here,' one of these guys said. 'In public like this. But since it's been set up we'll carry on with it. If anyone comes up to us and asks what's going on you'd better say you're trying to buy a shop off us and Simon's checking that everything's legal.'

'OK,' I replied. I understood his concern. Simon was pretty well known as the local bobby in this area of P—.

'So,' said one of the Special Branch men, 'what can we do for you?'

We gave them a brief outline of our story. We got the feeling they already knew a bit about it.

'We're not happy at all,' Zena said, 'with this situation we're in now. We've got these new identities, but without previous histories or references it's impossible for us to get jobs. We're also very worried about this flat we've been put in. It's a security risk.'

'What were you expecting to happen?'

'Exactly what we were told would happen,' she replied. 'They were going to set us up with a place, they were going to give us funds to get ourselves sorted out, we were going to have a history so that we can live as normal people.

That's what we expected from them. Not to be left down here, with nothing, on our own.'

'You understand,' I chipped in, 'there's no way I can start looking for work if I haven't got the references – the history.'

'Couldn't you make some up?'

'That wouldn't work. Even if I got a job, as soon as I started they'd find out I'd got false references and I'd be fired on the spot.'

OK, they said. When we went for jobs, we could use our new names, dates of birth and NI numbers. Then, when it came to the previous experience part, we'd have to say, 'I can't give you any previous history, but what I can do is give you the number of a high-ranking police officer who'll vouch for us.'

Great. It was pretty obvious to me that if I was called up for an interview and came out with that I was just going to be told to get lost.

Nonetheless, we put it to the test. We bought the local paper for a month and I phoned and applied for about forty jobs. These were straightforward manual work, hotel portering, kitchen hand, nothing that I wouldn't stand a chance for. And on the phone, each time, I explained the position and quoted a version of what the officer had said. One employer slammed the phone down on me. Another asked if I was a crank. The rest of them refused an interview unless I could complete the application form. It was exactly as I'd imagined.

Sometimes when I've explained this situation to people in authority they've said: Why didn't you just make something up, or go to the interview, get them on your side and then mention the police officer bit?

But we'd talked about this between ourselves. We really didn't think we could risk going to an interview, where our faces would be seen, and then come out with this line about the high-ranking police officer. If that had happened a few times, obviously we'd have become factory gossip, then pub gossip, then the word was just going to spread and spread.

'So why have this northerner and this Asian lass got this Special Branch officer vouching for them?' people'd say. 'What kind of folk get protected by Special Branch? Supergrasses? Murderers? Who are they? What have they done? Where are they from?' And so on. In the situation we were in we couldn't risk that.

The only other way I can describe what our situation was like is this: Imagine that I took your wallet now, your credit cards, driving licence, passport, birth certificate, and so on. Then I put you in a car and drove you to a new town, two hundred miles away, say, stuck you in a bedsit, and said, 'Right, this is who you are, you cannot use any of your previous jobs, or schools, or qualifications, or any other contacts or references you've got. You cannot even use your family. Start afresh.' How easy d'you think you'd find it? Believe me, you'd have problems just getting welfare, let alone a job.

And that's before you consider the ordeal we'd just come through. Our mental state was not good. It was hard enough to keep a sane conversation going between ourselves, let alone trying to convince an employer that we were 'normal people' who could put in a good day's work.

After a month or so of trying to get a job without references we went back to the Special Branch officers and explained what had happened. It wasn't working. Was there no way, we asked, that their organization could now complete the deal, give us the second half of these new identities – the references and personal histories – so that the case could be closed and we could get on with our lives?

No, they said. We'd had all that was coming to us. There was nothing more they could do. Fair enough. We were not their problem. Good taxpayers' money had gone into giving us the new ID, we had that, and they'd offered to vouch for us. What more were they expected to do? One

212

thing I will say for the Special Branch is that they never let us down; they never promised to do anything they subsequently couldn't deliver.

ZENA:

As well as asking these Special Branch officers to help us get a history we'd also brought up the question of moving from Waterworks Row. It wasn't just the fleas, and the cold, and the stench from the sewage works; the location was a definite security risk.

The trains that ran at the back of the house every hour, on the hour, were so near that the cupboards and table would rattle. It was pitch-dark outside in that lane. As Jack said, all someone would have to do was come down there at night, park a car round the corner, wait for a train to come by, give a kick to that rotten door and it would have gone through. They could have been up the stairs, have done the dirty deed and be gone and nobody would have known.

One night there was a loud banging on our front door. We ran to the window. It was the lad from the flat at the back of the cottage. He was limping and holding his leg.

'Could I use your phone, please?' he asked. He'd had an accident on his motorbike.

'Come in, mate,' said Jack. So he came in and phoned the police. He needed to report the accident. It was an hour and a half before anyone turned up. The police sergeant who came had been unable to find the address.

'I didn't even know these cottages existed,' he said. 'And I've been in the force thirty years.'

That little incident hardly reassured us.

Special Branch had made it quite clear that they couldn't help us, either with references or a move, so we made an appointment to see a housing officer from a group called the Three Oaks Housing Association. She was a brisk, business-suited lady. The stern expression on her face didn't bode well. We'd already decided that if we were going to get any kind of priority, we'd have to tell her our whole story.

'Well,' she said when we'd finished. 'I'll need confirmation of this. I can't put you on the list without that. We get all kinds of tales told to us in here, you know.' She would need, she said, at least a letter of approval from the police in Lincolnshire, giving our names and a full statement of exactly what we'd been through. We explained the situation: that Lincolnshire had told us to say nothing. That wasn't relevant, she said. She needed a letter. Otherwise we couldn't go on the list, let alone get priority.

So we were forced to ring Alan Jones in Lincoln and ask him to contact this lady for us.

'You were told not to reveal your circumstances to anybody,' he said.

'I know,' Jack said, 'but it's the only way we can get on her list. She insists on confirmation.'

'I'm sorry,' Alan replied. 'I can't do that for you.'

Jack pointed out that originally, at the meeting he'd had when we'd first moved to P—, we had been promised there would be someone from Housing to sort us out, and that contact had never materialized. But Alan still couldn't help. He was sorry, it was out of his hands, but he'd been told by his superiors that we were no longer Lincolnshire police's problem. He was unable to give us the confirmation we needed.

We went back home and reviewed our situation. What could we do? We were banging our heads against a brick wall. We decided, eventually, that we'd go and put our case to our local MP, George Draper. It was the first time we'd tried to get help from such a high-ranking man as this.

'So what can I do for you?' he asked, when we were sitting in front of the long desk in his office. He was in his late middle-age, grey-haired, very distinguished-looking and well spoken, as if he'd seen a lot of life, but from the point of view where he'd been used to telling people what to do.

'We've got to be sure,' Jack said, 'that whatever we tell you now is going to stay with yourself and go no further.'

'No, it will go no further,' he reassured us.

'It's quite an unusual story.'

'I've heard just about everything in my time.'

We looked at each other. 'I don't think you're ever going to have heard anything quite like this,' said Jack.

So he sat and listened, and at the end said again, 'So how can I help you?'

We explained what we needed: a letter from him to this DCI Russell in Lincoln asking him to verify our circumstances to the housing association lady.

'OK,' he said, 'I'll do that for you.'

The next thing we knew, PC Alan Jones was on the phone. 'How come you've approached your MP?' he asked.

'We rang you, Alan,' I replied (I'd been first to the phone). 'We tried to get you to help us. You wouldn't, so we had no other option. We need to get out of here. It isn't safe.'

Alan didn't sound very happy with this at all. But finally, in August, a letter came through from Lincoln to the housing association. It was two lines long and referred to Michael Burnley and Sonya Atkinson. 'These people and their circumstances are known to us,' it read. 'If any further information is required, please contact DCI Russell.' The Lincoln police knew we had new identities. What harm, we thought, would have come from them merely verifying our situation?

Meanwhile this housing lady had tried to get our case moved to the council. The council had returned us to her. She'd sent us back to the council – and finally, after three attempts to offload us, she'd been forced actually to visit us at the cottage.

This two-line letter seemed to have really upset her. She

walked in and threw it down on the table. 'This is disgusting,' she said, 'wasting my time like this.'

We just sat there, gobsmacked. We didn't know what to say.

'Now I'm going to have to sit here,' she went on, 'and take your story down. I'm going to have to cancel another appointment and waste yet more time on this . . .' That was the way she was talking. It was as if it was our fault that this letter was so brief and inadequate, that the names were wrong. Eventually she got round to jotting down a few details of our story.

'So d'you think we'll be eligible for a move?' I asked.

'I'll have to look into it.'

I mentioned that one of the Special Branch officers had already told us to avoid one district of P— because it was notoriously racist; there were National Front based there and so on. So, naturally, I brought this up.

'That's ridiculous,' she said. 'There's no racism in P—. The only instance of racism I can ever recall here was a Nigerian tenant of ours who got pelted with eggs on the street.' It was clear she didn't think that was a particularly big deal. We just looked at each other as if to say 'What is this woman *on*?'

But she took our statement and told us she'd get back to us.

'Like hell you will,' Jack said to me as she drove off.

We didn't think she would and we were right; we've never heard another thing from her.

JACK:

It goes without saying that these meetings and phone calls were the high points of our life. We couldn't afford to give up hoping that somehow things would come right. But most of our time that second summer was spent indoors, doing the same old things as before, watching TV, having occasional squabbles, brewing up fantasies, and so on.

We were basically just passing the days staring either at the TV or out of the window, going to bed knowing we were going to wake up and do exactly the same thing we had done the day before, the day before that, the week before that, the month before that, and the month before that. Anyone who's been unemployed for a short time and stayed in for a week or two and watched daytime TV will understand how it was.

Everything seemed so much more depressing that summer. The year before we'd had Dennis and Margaret and Alan coming down to visit us from time to time. There'd been all the hope of the new identity, the new future. Now we'd got our new names, but Frank and Beth Clayton were going nowhere because the identities weren't complete. We were in limbo and there was, it seemed, nobody out there who gave a damn about us.

The flat was cramped and dingy. Whatever we did to try and clean it up, it always seemed to revert to being a hole. The trains continued to thunder by every hour, rattling the teacups on the table, and on hot days the sewage works filled the air with a noxious stench.

Even in high summer it was dark and cold in that place. Zena, more often than not, would sit huddled in a blanket. She was so quiet and subdued. The old spirit and life seemed to have been leeched out of her. Only on these occasional meetings with Special Branch or whoever did she seem to fire up again, become for an hour or so her old self.

As well as phoning up jobs from the local paper I tried to get casual work by calling into places locally. I got friendly with Mick, the bloke who ran the scrapyard. Then there was a sawmill up the road. But they all had their local mates who'd come in and help out when things were busy. There was a lot of unemployment in P—, and plenty of guys who were available for a bit of cash work when it came along. There just wasn't room for someone new, especially someone new with no history.

I felt as if I'd been knocking on doors all my life. It was only seeing Zena, hunched there in front of the telly, that kept me going. I just wasn't going to allow us to get ground down. Somehow we would get ourselves out of this situation. We would be a normal couple. With jobs and a home. Would we ever be able to have kids? It seemed too distant a dream even to contemplate.

We had rung the housing association lady after a couple of weeks of waiting, but she'd been unavailable and eventually we decided there was going to be no joy from that department. There was nothing for it but to get back in touch with the Special Branch boys. Ask them whether they would be prepared to speak on our behalf to someone in the DSS. I had the idea that perhaps we could make the move another way. Get a grant or loan from them to relocate. If the Housing people wouldn't help, we could do it ourselves.

To cut a long and frustrating couple of months short, the Special Branch did agree to help us. An officer spoke on our behalf to the DSS. Our MP, Mr Draper, also agreed to write a letter for us. Finally the DSS allowed us a relocation loan of £600. It would have to be paid back weekly out of our dole but it was more than enough for us to make the move, out of this insecure dump we'd been squatting in for eight months.

Where would we go?

With a burst of enthusiasm we decided we'd leave P— altogether. We'd head back up north and make a fresh start. The people were friendlier up there, we reckoned.

We weren't, obviously, going to go anywhere near our home town. But on the other side of the country we thought we'd be OK. We had an idea of a place on the north-east coast. Somewhere like Scarborough, where I might more easily stand a chance of getting casual work, particularly in summer. The other point was that we'd be nearer to my mother, whose condition wasn't getting any better.

So we bought train tickets and made a rapid tour of the

north-east. We spent a couple of nights in York, a couple more in Scarborough. But the rents were too high for us and, without jobs or references, the agents were insisting on three months in advance. Even with our quite substantial loan it wasn't going to be possible. We headed back to P—.

What with the train fares and the B and Bs, we realized that we now only had barely enough to secure a property locally.

17

JACK:
Luckily PC Chalker knew the guy who owned the post office in the middle of this village-suburb we'd settled in. He had a flat next to his shop which he'd been renting out to three students he was now evicting on account, apparently, of their rowdiness and generally filthy habits.

It was bigger than 6a Waterworks Row, and also, more importantly, in a much more secure position, in the centre of the village, overlooking this little green, with people passing back and forth at all times. It would have been much harder for anyone finding us to attack us or try to do us in on the quiet. If we'd put up a fight it was central enough that somebody would have noticed.

We'd had a look over this place once, in the evening, and it had seemed fine. A student dive, obviously enough, but nothing that couldn't be fixed with a broom, some Jif and a few J-cloths. When we actually moved in it was a different story. We couldn't believe the state they'd left it in. Presumably as an act of revenge for being thrown out they'd just trashed the place. The Young Ones couldn't have done better. They'd pissed on the carpets, shat on top of the wardrobes. In among all the junk and crap I found a couple of orange fliers which read THE FINAL FRY. It had the names of these lads who'd lived there, then, *We're being evicted, come to the final fry. All welcome.*

I've been in some pretty squalid holes in my time but this truly was the worst. It even made Mrs Grimes's look clean. As we were knee-deep in rubbish, cleaning up, I found a jawbone.

'Look,' I said to Zena, 'I've just found a jawbone.' It was funny, because it didn't surprise either of us.

The smell of stale urine was so bad that for the first three weeks, in the middle of December, we had to keep the windows open all day, otherwise you felt as if you'd throw up. In the bathroom the toilet was covered in shit, right down to the carpet, which squelched and stank. We tore that out, and the ones in the bathroom and bedroom.

It took us months to get the place properly clean. We didn't have a settee or a bed for the first six weeks we were there. We slept on a futon we'd borrowed from the landlord of the pub.

ZENA:

When we'd finally got this flat cleaned up, and we were into New Year, we thought, Right, let's try and leave the bad old days behind and get into village life. We really wanted to make friends, because that's one thing we'd cut ourselves off from totally – friends. All we'd had, for the two years since we'd run away, had been each other, day in, day out. We just longed to be part of a community again, to have people we could stop and chat to in the street. Women for me to talk to, and men for Jack.

So we decided to spend some of the money we usually put aside for bills making friends with our new neighbours. We'd go down to the pub one or two evenings a week and sit up at the bar and try and join in.

It was fine to start with. The people from round about seemed genuinely interested in us, asking questions about where we were from, how we'd got down here, how we'd met and were together. 'Didn't your parents mind you getting married?' they used to ask. So I stuck to the story I'd made up when we were first trying to get a place: that I'd lost my mother and father in a car crash in Pakistan; that I'd been adopted by a white family and become Westernized; that my dad was a caterer with a big business

221

in the north; that I'd met Jack like that. (It was the hardest thing for me to say that both my parents had died.)

'Oh yes,' they'd say. 'When you tell us that you can see you've had a good upbringing.' I used to keep my thoughts to myself but that frequent remark really used to get to me. They were being racist without even realizing it!

'So where have you moved from?' they would ask.

'Oh, we've been doing a lot of travelling,' we used to reply. Or, 'We've moved down from Derbyshire to find work.'

'So what d'you do for a living?'

We'd just been on the move, we said. Now we were looking for work.

It was all fine at first. We made friends in the village. I did a bit of babysitting for the landlady of the pub. We talked about me doing a curry night for them. I even cooked them a sample curry.

But then, as people realized we were pretty permanently on the dole, they started gossiping about us. Soon they were calling us scroungers and criticizing our every move. If we stayed in we were keeping a low profile; if we went out we were spending too much. They even used to moan about where I went shopping in town. If I came home from my weekly trip with a Marks and Spencer's bag it would be, 'How come she can afford to shop at Marks, they're on the bloody dole?'

We knew these things were being said because our friend the pub landlady kept us informed. Quite often we'd over-hear it directly. People would come out of the post office and talk about us in loud voices right under our window. 'There's a couple live up there, she's a Pakistani, they're from the north, they never go out, they're on the dole, they're scroungers.' All that sort of thing.

It got to the point where we'd hear them laughing down-stairs if we got up late in the morning. As I got out of bed the floorboards would creak and then their conversation

222

would go quiet and you'd hear them giggling. I took to tiptoeing across the room when I got up.

Then there were the little racist jibes. We were sitting in the pub one evening talking about culture and religion and this man from the village laughed and said, 'Oh well, round here we always used to call Pakistanis "Pakis".' I had a glass in my hand and I just thought, Shall I or shan't I? In the end I slammed down my drink and we just walked out of there.

Our two years on the run had changed me. Before, back home, I'd have bitten my tongue in the face of a remark like that. Now I couldn't seem to help myself.

It wasn't everyone in the village who was like this. There were two young couples who were different: a pair of young professionals, Tom and Rosie, and another young couple from London, Steve and Rachel.

Our real problems started, though, when we came back from our respite on the Isle of Wight.

JACK:
It's another protracted tale as to how we managed to get away for this short holiday. As autumn had come round to winter, and we'd both started going down with numerous illnesses again, I'd said to Dr Gill that what I thought Zena really needed for her health was a complete break. From the stress of our daily circumstances. Not just the constant fear, but the more mundane worry of making ends meet on twenty-five pounds a week. (After we'd put aside money for bills and repayment of our relocation loan, that was what we were living on.)

'I think,' said Dr Gill, 'that what you're referring to is a respite.' There was an officially sanctioned break that you could apply for and he, our medical adviser, was prepared to support us. He wrote a letter for us saying that our physical and mental state was being compounded by the stress we were facing, and so on, and I took this down to the DSS.

We were refused on the grounds that we weren't a high enough priority. Three months before I'd never even heard of a respite, but knowing that it was now at least a possibility, and knowing also what kind of state Zena was in, I decided to fight the decision all the way. Eventually, after being kicked back by ever-more senior officers, I travelled over to the Independent Review Service in Birmingham, sat there and went through our story for five hours to one official, before being refused by another official I wasn't even allowed to meet.

I tried to get one of the officers from Special Branch to help. 'I can't do that,' he said. 'There'd be too many pointed questions.' What he meant I have absolutely no idea, but he made it clear that that avenue was closed. I tried a solicitor, who suggested we apply to the Lord Chancellor. But we were refused legal aid on the grounds that what we were applying for – the respite money – was less than what it would cost to fight for it.

So we went back to our MP, George Draper, and asked him if he would write on our behalf to the Lord Chancellor and Peter Lilley. He refused to write to the Social Security minister but wrote on our behalf to the Lord Chancellor. In due course a letter came back saying, in so many words, that the Lord Chancellor was sitting high up on his fence and wouldn't come down for anybody.

Zena then had the idea that we should go back and ask Mr Draper, as he was a Labour MP, if he might contact Tony Blair for us. His refusal was almost like a sketch from a comedy show.

'Would you like to come in?' said his assistant. We walked in to the far end of the room, and there was our MP, as before, behind his huge desk.

'Right,' he said, 'so what can I do for you now?'

'We'd like you to arrange an appointment for us to see Tony Blair.'

'And what d'you think he can do for you?'

'Well,' Zena began, 'we don't know, but we thought if we could just see him he might be sympathetic to our situation and might be able to help us.'

'No,' said Mr Draper. Just the one word, accompanied by a shake of the head.

'Well, could we see an adviser to Mr Blair?' Zena began.

'No,' he said. 'Right, thank you very much.' He looked back at his papers and his assistant made the sign that it was time for us to leave. The whole thing must have taken about thirty seconds from start to finish.

All these setbacks took their toll on our home life. We were so frustrated with everything and everybody outside that sometimes the only place for our anger to go was towards each other.

The other thing that drove me crazy at this time was being called in for Restarts. By mid-March I'd been signing on at the same office for a year and so I'd get called in and put in front of some sixteen-year-old who'd say, 'You should really be working now, Mr Clayton, you've been unemployed for a full year, have you thought of the following ways of trying to get a job?' And I'd want to grab hold of them and scream, 'Listen, mush, the Special Branch won't give me references or a history so I *can't* get a job.'

But obviously, once again, I'd have to bite my tongue and say, 'Can I see the manager, please?'

'I'm sorry, the manager's not available at the moment.'

'Well, could I see the supervisor, please?'

And so on.

Our records there contained no details of our circumstances. The contact I'd met during that hurried lunchtime meeting with Dennis and Alan when we'd first arrived in P— a year before had emigrated. There wasn't even a note on our file. In the end I had to brief a new supervisor.

Finally, miraculously, after five more months of fighting for our respite we struck lucky with a marvellous woman from the social services. Debbie Jones immediately agreed to release money for new clothing that we badly needed, and for a respite.

It was June by now, high summer. We decided we'd go, for a week, back to where we'd been happiest since we left home – the Isle of Wight. We stayed in a B and B in Sandown, not far from where we'd been before. The old place had stopped being a B and B, but we went to one just down the road.

Although the island brought back strong memories at first, we soon relaxed enough to have a lovely time. It did cross our minds to call on Brenda Steele and confront her about the missing money. But we decided that that was in the past and best left. We didn't want to spoil out hard-fought-for break.

The respite money enabled us to do loads of things barred to us before. We went to the pictures, to restaurants, to a waxworks. We took a bus to the Needles. It did us the world of good. It really was like having your batteries recharged.

But when we came back to the village we immediately noticed a change. We were passing people we knew in the street, saying 'hello' and they were blanking us. What on earth is going on? we thought.

On our second night back we decided we'd go down to the pub. Just to tell people what a great time we'd had and let them know we were back. We walked into that bar and it was unbelievable – everybody moved away from us. I said to Joyce the landlady, 'Bloody hell, if this place were a ship it would capsize.' Because the whole of the village was at one end of the room and Zena and I were at the other.

Joyce just laughed it off. 'Oh, take no notice,' she said. But this escalated. The next day I went into the post office. 'What is going on?' I asked Desmond.

'I think what you want to do,' he replied, 'is you want to be careful. A lot of people have been coming in here and saying, you know, "Bloody hell, I'm going to give up my job. They've been on holiday and they're not even working."'

I flipped. Totally. I leant over the counter and looked him straight in the eye. 'Look, mate,' I said. 'You can tell them, when they come in here, that I live next door. That I've got a big bloody baseball bat and I don't give a shit who they are, I'll cave their bloody heads in. The first arsehole I hear talking about us like that, they're going to get it.'

Back home I'd always been one to talk my way out of trouble. But now I could feel my aggression rising. It was like a fire inside me I couldn't control. With Zena, sometimes, I'd flare up over the stupidest little things. Then later, when I'd calmed down, I'd think, What was all that about? It scared me at times, the way I'd changed.

And for a while afterwards, when I went into the shop, Desmond was very polite. 'Hello,' or 'Good morning,' he'd say. 'Thank you.' It was respect. As my brother Ryan always used to say, 'There's some people you can talk nicely to, and some people you can't.'

My outburst didn't stop the village tittle-tattle, though. I decided I'd go and see Steve and Rachel, our friends from London. He was Cockney but she was more Cockney–Jewish, dark-haired and very statuesque in build.

I knocked on the door and Steve answered. 'Ah, Frank, mate, come on in. What can I do for you?'

I explained our situation. 'As you know, we've only been away a short time, and here we are back, and it's like everyone's just blanking us. No one's talking to us at all. What's going on?'

Rachel was lying there on the sofa and she just suddenly came out with this absolutely venomous stream of vitriol. 'Well what d'you *expect*? You're not even *working*, are you? You go off on holiday and then you're back and you're rubbing people's noses in it, coming back here with your suntans, sitting in the pub saying what a marvellous time you had. And all the time you're on the bloody *dole*.'

I sat there in shock. I was hearing this from someone I'd thought was a close friend of ours. Right, I thought, there's two ways I can go about this: I can jump all over her head and get arrested, or I can stay cool and walk out. Steve was looking at me as if he was expecting me to break his nose and then start on her.

I surprised myself. I stood up and very calmly I said, 'Rachel, I'm very disappointed in you. I'd thought of you as a good friend of ours. I've noticed that you've got a brand new car parked outside. Presumably you've got rent to pay here, and though you're both lucky enough to be working I don't ask you how you manage it because it's none of my bloody business. And I wouldn't dream of going round making snide remarks about you if you happened to be unfortunate enough to get the sack. If that's your opinion you're entitled to it, but I'm absolutely appalled and disgusted.'

Steve gave me a very apologetic look.

'I'm going,' I said. I walked out and he followed me to the porch.

'Sorry, mate,' he said. 'That was totally out of order.'

'Just forget it, all right.' I walked off. I was boiling with rage.

ZENA:
No one talked to us in the village after that. When we came back from that respite that was it. There was only one couple who stood by us: Tom and Rosie, the two young professionals. Rosie even made the effort to come round and see me one evening. 'It's hard when we're living in the village as well,' she said, 'but I just want you to know that Tom and I don't stand by any of what's being said. As far as we're concerned we're your friends, and that's the way we want it to stay.' But they were having problems of their own, with their neighbours, so they decided to sell up and leave.

228

The people in this place were just so backward. When I first opened my mouth in that pub they expected me to talk with an Asian accent. When I spoke in full-on Yorkshire they couldn't believe it.

Then our landlord, Desmond, when I went into the post office to cash the giro, smacked down the money on the surface almost as if it was his. 'I'm keeping you,' he told Jack one day. 'I'm keeping you both with my taxes.'

As for Rachel, who we'd thought was our friend, she turned out to be one vicious woman. She even went so far as to claim that I was having an affair, with this young lad from the village who had a girlfriend. When I heard that I couldn't believe it.

It hurt, it really hurt. They didn't even have the balls to come up and say it to your face. It was all done in that horrible quiet snidey way where it all sits underground.

JACK:
I didn't care so much about myself. I was thirty-five and hardly likely to become a rocket scientist. But Zena still had a chance. There were a thousand and one things she could do.

I wasn't prepared to see a young lass who was so bright and attractive and had so much to give as Zena just ground down in this way, to the point where she was sitting on the welfare state, losing self-respect, barely making ends meet, being suffocated in this awful narrow-minded little village we'd ended up in.

I decided it was time, despite all the risks, to try telling our story publicly. We'd gone as far as we could on our own. We weren't going to get any more help from the Old Bill, from Victim Support, from the DSS, from any of the organizations that are supposed to be there for people in trouble. The system just wasn't geared up for a case like ours.

So I went back up to see our MP, Mr Draper. He was

unavailable, I was told. I spoke to his assistant, Simon Cohen. A week later he got back to me. Mr Draper was not a publicity-seeking politician, he explained, so therefore was unable to help us. All I was asking was that he back us up, make the statement we'd prepared for the newspapers seem less like something from two nutters out of the blue. He was the only person with any clout who could help us. Obviously I couldn't go to the Special Branch boys or the police because they'd scream blue murder if they knew that the tale of their serial incompetence was about to come out.

'What I'm prepared to do for you,' Simon Cohen said eventually, 'is write a covering letter for you from this office, saying that we are aware of your circumstances and if they want to get in touch with me this statement is a fair and true account of what's happened to you.'

We were grateful for that. We fired off three statements to the *Guardian*, *The Times* and the *Daily Express*. We didn't bother with the tabloids, we wanted to go with somebody reputable who we could trust.

It was just twenty lines, handwritten, giving a basic outline of what had happened to us, saying we were still on the run. There were no names, no address, no mention of Special Branch.

Four weeks later we heard back from Simon. A senior editor at the *Daily Express*, Brian Talbot, wanted to talk to us.

I phoned. Talbot sounded, to be frank, like a total idiot. He *might* be interested, he said, but there was absolutely no way there would be any money involved.

'Look,' I pleaded, 'you must have gathered from our statement that we're at the end of the road here. We're in desperate straits and we're trying to find financial assistance to get us relocated. If you're interested in the story, surely you could find your way to paying us something.'

He addressed me then as if I should be honoured that he was taking thirty seconds of his precious time to speak to me. His last offer was that I could take it or leave it. Publicity on his terms without payment, or nothing. I talked it over with Zena and, desperate though we were, we decided to leave it. We had the very worst of gut feelings about Mr Talbot.

We had, it seemed to me, tried everybody. For days I just sat there thinking, That's it, we've reached the end of the road, there's no one else to turn to.

Then, one night, I was staring over at the bookshelf in the flat, and my eyes settled on the four books we'd saved up, over the two years we'd been in the village, to buy: the three by the hostages – Terry Waite, Brian Keenan, John McCarthy and Jill Morrell – plus Andy McNab's *Bravo Two Zero*, another inspiring story of a guy who'd lived through terrible danger and hardship and survived.

Surely, I was thinking, with a sudden surge of excitement, if anybody was going to understand our situation, it would be one of these men. Perhaps we could write to them. I suggested the idea to Zena.

'Well, we could,' she said. 'But I don't think they'd reply. They must get hundreds of letters, being famous like that.'

'It's worth a try,' I replied. And after discussing it we decided to try John McCarthy first.

So, fired up with one mad last hope, I contacted our MP's assistant again. He agreed to write a confirmation letter, and we sent off a brief statement of our circumstances to John McCarthy.

'We've got nothing to lose,' I said, as I sealed up the letter.

18

JACK:
My mother's illness had now progressed to the stage where she'd soon, Jenny said, have to go back into hospital. I was so worried about her that I decided I had to go back home and see her.

I stayed with my brother Ryan and called on Ma in her new flat. She was still dreadfully upset about everything that had happened. Very frightened for her own safety. Horrified by the continuing death threats not just to us, but to Jenny and her children. She was unable to understand how there was no redress for us, in England, in the 1990s. Or why the police couldn't help us. (Even though she'd refused to press her own charges against the brothers for fear of further trouble.) Nor could she see that there was ever going to be a resolution.

She was worried about me staying too long in the city, so I said my goodbyes and hitched back to Zena.

Two months later Ryan phoned to tell me she'd been rushed into hospital and might have only days to live. It was late on a Friday. I couldn't get a travel warrant till the DSS office reopened, and the doctor had told me that Ma's condition was stable, so I decided I'd get up there first thing on the Monday – a decision I regret bitterly now. On the Monday morning at six o'clock the phone rang.

It's funny how they say you know these things. Of course it was a highly unusual time for us to get a call, but the first ring of that phone filled the bedroom like a gong and I knew Ma was dead. It was the weirdest thing, impossible to put into words, but it was almost as if she was there for a split second with me, in the room – and then gone. It was almost like a sharp intake of breath, as I sat bolt upright in the bed.

'Are you all right?' Zena asked, even before she'd gone to pick up the phone.

'Yeah.'

She ran downstairs and I heard her say, 'Oh – God – no.' I didn't need to be told that Ma had died. After I'd held Zena tight in my arms for a minute or more I walked in a daze into the bathroom and once again I found myself staring into the mirror above the sink.

'You've got to be strong now,' I told myself. 'You can't crack, you can't crumble, because if you do that's it, you're going to be finished.'

We had a coffee and I walked alone down the icy pavements to the DSS office. It was just before nine, and I was the first one there.

I saw this guy called McCready, a grey-haired Scottish fellow who had dealt with most of our claims and knocked us back for just about everything we'd applied for. But today he seemed to be putting up the truce flag. When he heard my news he nodded sympathetically and sorted out a travel warrant which would cover tickets for us both to go home.

'Right,' I said to Zena, 'let's get our bags packed.' We were on the first available train.

I notified Special Branch that we were going. I had to, because Zena was coming. She wanted to pay her respects to Ma. Nor did she want a repeat of the first time I'd left her alone, when half the young lads in the village had taken advantage of my absence to run past smacking the windows and doors of our flat and shouting racist abuse.

We stayed at Jenny's house. I waited three days before I visited Ma in the Chapel of Rest. I didn't want to see her laid out on a slab in the morgue. Jenny and I went up there together and paid our respects one by one.

'I'm really sorry for not being there, Ma,' I whispered

to her, and tears streamed down my cheeks as I sat by her there, still as a marble statue among the flowers. 'I'm really sorry you had to die on your own.'

None of the family had been with her, because the hospital had made a cock-up with the telephone numbers. So for that stupid reason she had been alone.

Almost the hardest part was going back to her flat to tidy up. Ryan and my sisters had sorted out most of her possessions. My job was to sort out and bag up her clothes. It was only while I was doing this that I realized how terribly scared she must have been, all those months, now years, we'd been on the run. Because everywhere I went in that flat there were knives. There were knives in drawers, knives by the side of her bed, knives under towels in cupboards – they were everywhere.

When I found them I just wept. Right there in the flat like a child. While I'd always had Zena with me, Ma had just been there alone, terrified that they were going to come back and try something more serious next time.

We had the funeral and went straight home. We were putting Jenny and her children at risk by staying. Not that Zena's family were likely to have known that Ma had passed on. And believe me, had they dared show their faces at the crematorium they'd have been dead meat as far as Ryan and Dan were concerned. But as soon as the ceremony was over, obviously we had to go.

As we sped home in the train I barely spoke. I stared out of the train window at the dull grey sky, the few tatters of brown and yellow leaves still clinging to the branches of trees swaying in the strong November wind. My head was swirling with emotion. God forbid, I was thinking, that Zena should ever have to go through that same pain of not being able to say goodbye properly. By running away to marry me, already she'd missed out on so much, just as her dad and her family had missed out on so much. I'd always said to her, 'Zena, your father does not switch off twenty years of loving, just like that.' What father could? Whatever he said, I knew he must still love her, just as I loved her. And I was sure that her mother and all the rest of her family loved and cared for her too.

I knew they thought what they were doing was right. But I thought what we were doing was right, too. Because I loved Zena and couldn't imagine life without her.

What we'd done wasn't wrong. We'd fallen in love and got married, we hadn't committed a crime. It was so bloody sad that this was happening. Just seeing my mother lying there, dead, her life, with all its hardships and deprivations, finally over, had made me realize how terribly short life is. I'd missed out on those three final years of her life, and she'd missed out on seeing Zena and me married and happy.

Is this the way it has to be? I was asking myself, over and over. Is this the way it has to go on being? That we have to waste what is left of our lives hating each other?

ZENA:

Jack's mum was somebody I loved as much as my own family. She'd always been somebody who'd never had a bad word to say about me, from the first day I met her onwards. She was always happy to call me 'daughter', even with all the trouble I brought.

We'd always discussed what we'd do if she died, and we'd long before decided that we'd both go home to pay our respects. If my family were to show their faces, we thought, we'd deal with it. It was not as if we'd be alone, or in a position where they could do anything to us that they could get away with. We'd told Special Branch what we were doing.

Even so, as I was standing beside Jack in the little chapel at the crematorium I was praying that they hadn't found out, wouldn't be so stupid as to turn up. I knew only too well that if they had heard, there was a strong chance that they might appear. I was worried not just for us, but for

Jenny and her children. God knows what chaos might have ensued.

But we'll never know if they did find out because as soon as the funeral was over we were back on that train and home.

When Jack searched her flat he found that she'd destroyed everything to do with both of us: the letters we'd written, the photographs, the bundle of notes I'd dropped down to him from my gable-end window. She must have been frightened that if my brothers had come back and found all this it would have caused extra trouble. That, and all the knives Jack discovered, made us realize how terribly scared she'd been.

For days, Jack didn't say anything about his mother's death at all. He never even cried. Then on the Saturday night he went out for a drink on his own. He was gone a long while and I was worried he might come back drunk. But I'd never seen him in such a state as he was when he returned that time.

I was sitting up watching TV. He came in and immediately he started shouting, 'Those bastards, I'd like to make them fucking pay.'

Then he picked up a stool and hurled it against the wall, against this picture I'd bought when we'd moved from Waterworks Row, of a boat in the sunset by the sea. It cracked and fell to the floor. He went through into the kitchen. There was a glass plate on the top there. He threw that at the cupboards and I heard it just shatter everywhere. Then he came back in and now he was ranting about the people in the village.

'I'm going to get those bastards,' he was going. 'I'm going to fucking get them.'

I ran and stood in front of the door. 'You're drunk, love,' I said. 'Just go to bed.'

'Move out of the way, Zena,' he went. He used my real name, something he hadn't done since we got married.

'No, love,' I said, 'just calm down. Sit down now.'

I'd never seen him – or anyone – as drunk as this. I didn't know how to control it. He frightened the life out of me standing there like someone I didn't know, a stranger.

'I hope they fucking know,' he muttered (he'd switched back to my family now), 'what it feels like one day. What they put my mother through. I'm going to fucking show 'em,' he went on.

He crashed past me up the stairs. I heard him kick open the bathroom door and then I heard him fall. I ran up after him. He was sitting in the corner of the landing with his head in his hands.

'Oh, love,' I went, running over to him, 'what's up?'

'Don't you come near me.'

'No, love, it's all right . . .'

'Don't you come near me.'

'Come on, love, we'll get your coat off . . .'

'I don't want to be doing you any harm, Zena. Just go. Just go downstairs.'

'No, love, don't worry, you won't be doing me any harm.'

'Just go downstairs.'

Then he was sobbing again. 'I can hear Ma calling,' he was going.

I knelt down beside him and hugged him. 'Don't leave me,' he was sobbing. 'I couldn't lose you too.'

Eventually he got back up and went downstairs. He just sat there in the armchair for ages, with these glazed eyes, saying nothing. Then he was off again. 'I'm going to show them.' He was looking at me, and it was a look I'd never seen before. 'You're just like them, aren't you?' he said. 'You're one of them, taking their fucking side.'

'No, love, I'm not.'

'You are.'

Finally, after an hour or so, he'd calmed down enough for me to get him to bed. I pulled his shoes off and he fell asleep in his clothes. I lay beside him, sobbing. For the first time since we'd run away together I felt totally alone.

I'd left everything in the flat as it was because he'd told me once that that's what you have to do when people are drunk, because if you clean up after them they never understand what they've done.

And when he woke up in the morning he couldn't believe the mess he'd made.

I said, 'You said things to me last night I'll never ever forget.'

He was so sorry. 'I didn't mean them,' he said. 'Love, you've got to understand I didn't mean them.'

'I can understand,' I said, 'in a way, because you've built up this rage for so long. It had to come out sooner or later. But it's come out to the wrong person.'

'I know.'

It was Sunday, so we took a long walk down the river and out into the countryside. We went for a drink in a little pub by the riverside and we talked this all through.

'Listen,' I said, 'you're going to need to talk to somebody about what happened last night.'

'I know, love,' he said. 'I am so sorry.' He was in a terrible state about it; couldn't believe what he'd done and said. He would go to the doctor, he said, see if he couldn't find someone to talk to, help him.

On the very next day when we came down in the morning there was a long white envelope on the mat, addressed to us in black ink, a handwriting neither of us knew. It wasn't our MP or any of the other people we'd been dealing with. Jack picked it up.

'Well, open it up, love,' I said.

For some reason he wanted to take it into the kitchen to open it. I followed him in there and watched as he tore it open, peeling it back between thumb and forefinger, very slowly along the top. There was a single sheet of ivory paper inside.

'Bloody hell!' he said, as he pulled it out and opened it.

'What?'

'It's from John McCarthy.'

'Let's see, let's see!'

John McCarthy had read our letter and was appalled, he said, that such a thing could happen, in Britain, in the 1990s. He'd be in touch very soon, he went on, and in the meantime we must keep our spirits up and not despair.

The feeling was amazing. At last, a door had opened.

Epilogue

ZENA:

We've been able to tell our story now, and we've had some money for it, and, for the time being at least – thank God – we're no longer on the dole. We've moved away from the village and we have, at last, from time to time, some other people to talk to. Not just John, but our publishers, our agent, and others who have offered us help and advice.

I only wish I could say that the whole horror is over, that we're reconciled with my family; or even just that my family have removed the death threat, told us that they'll allow us to live together in peace. Or even that Special Branch have sorted out full new identities for us and that Frank and Beth Clayton are working away somewhere quietly in the UK, living their own lives.

But I can't. We're still in hiding, still living with the fear that one day they'll catch up with us. Jack still times my trips out to the shops. Even now we haven't unpacked our clothes. There are two big wardrobes in the flat we're in at the moment, but everything's still in bags at the side. That's just the mindset we've got into; we're always waiting, watching, scared inside.

Night-times are the worst. I just hate the silence. If a car pulls up outside you're straight up and over to the window, to see who it is. Every evening, last thing, Jack brings the baseball bat in from the lounge and puts it on the bedside table.

I'm not giving up. Most days we go out for a walk at some stage. Just to get us out of the house for an hour or two. We go along the river or up into town. For a while we took to going to a beautiful local church where it's quiet, and you can think. There's a postcard I found in a rack there, with an anonymous poem on it, that sums up how I feel.

Don't quit

When things go wrong as they sometimes will,
When the road you're trudging
Seems all uphill.
When the funds are low and the debts are high
And you want to smile but you have to sigh,
When care is pressing you down a bit,
Rest, if you must, but don't you quit.
Life is queer with its twists and turns,
As every one of us sometimes learns,
And many a failure turns about
When he might have won if he stuck it out;
Don't give up though the pace seems slow –
You may succeed with another blow.
Success is failure turned inside out –
The silver tint of the clouds of doubt,
And you never can tell how close you are,
It may be near when it seems so far;
So stick to the fight when you're hardest hit –
It's when things seem worst that
You must not quit.

JACK:

I was walking through the mall in the middle of town the other day, and I saw this guy in the distance, coming up towards me. It was obvious there was something wrong with him. He was talking and giggling to himself and clapping. People were walking past him and laughing at him.

I felt so sorry for him. Because there was something, somewhere along the line, that had made him flip. He wasn't born like that. He was somebody's son, somebody's brother. And as I walked on, I just thought to myself, Yeah, I can understand, because I've been so close to that precipice myself.

I've walked into shops and I've been so tense I've just wanted to scream. At anybody. The shop assistant. The other customers. I'm sure on more than one occasion when I've been coming down the hill from town, fired up from yet another setback, my lips have been moving and I've been muttering away to myself.

A few years ago, back home with my mates, I'd probably have been one of the ones laughing. But I didn't then. I just looked at that man and I thought, There, but for the grace of God . . .

John McCarthy and the people he has put us in touch with have saved us from the worst of a living hell. But our story still isn't over. In the nationwide Asian community Zena's photograph is, we have to assume, still circulating. The bounty hunter is still asking questions, still trying to get his fee. Are they still paying the private investigator, I wonder? How long is it before a chance encounter exposes us, before we wake one night to discover that the front door's gone through, that what we've feared for all this time is suddenly upon us?

This shouldn't be happening. Not here. This is supposed to be a country of cherished freedoms and hard-won free speech. All I've ever wanted is that I should be allowed to marry and live quietly with the woman I fell in love with. So why is it that we are still in hiding; still, daily, in fear of our lives?

ZENA:
I think about my family a lot. There are certain times when I yearn to see them all. I long to put my arms around them and hold them, especially the children. I was very close to my sister's daughter, my little niece, Mina. I loved her as if she were my own.

It would be wonderful if one day they could come to terms with our marriage, remove this death threat from us and have us back. But at the same time, with all the lies they've told us, I think we'd find it very hard to trust them now. Because they could always say they'd accepted it, and then, at a later stage, do what they wanted with us. That's how Asian communities work. They're patient, they're prepared to bide their time.

There have been times when I've woken up happy and then suddenly remembered what's happened and felt like closing my eyes and hoping I never wake up again. I just want the nightmare to go away; of these people, my own family, hunting us down to a point where I feel we're going to be looking over our shoulders for the rest of our lives.

But I don't regret for one minute the decision I made, that night, lying on my bed staring at the ceiling, in mental turmoil. It was the right decision. I loved Jack then but over our four years on the run that love has only strengthened and deepened. We've had our squabbles and arguments – and that one dreadful night after his mum's funeral – but all in all he's been everything I ever wanted. He said he would put his life on the line for me, and he has done. And he's fought, that's the thing I admire most about him, he's a fighter, he never gives up. Where would we be today if he had, somewhere along the line, just crumbled?

The very first time I saw him I knew then that I loved him. Something just clicked. People say there's no such thing as falling in love with somebody straight away but I did with Jack. Why? It's impossible to describe. He's caring, obviously. He's a modern man: he can cook and clean and – with a bit of prompting – always does his fair share. He makes me laugh; even when I've been in my saddest times he's always made me laugh. He's patient with me; if something's up with me he'll sit there and try and understand what's wrong, what I'm trying to say. Sometimes when I'm down, he just knows, I don't have to say anything. But none of this is why I love him; there's something there I can't explain in words – that just makes him Jack.

In our religion the day you're born it's already written who you should marry. I truly believe that this was meant to be – I was already written for Jack. When I look at him now and think of my love for him I can't see how it could be any other way.

JACK:

I can honestly say there has never been a point when I've thought, I wish we'd never left. To be with Zena I had to go – so that was that. Once she'd come into my life I couldn't imagine life without her. It wasn't just that she was so attractive, and such a lovely person – from the start I was able to communicate with her in a way that I've never done with other women. Which is strange, because we come from such poles apart.

She's really had to toughen up these last four years. Widen up, become streetwise, call it what you want. It was that or become a nervous wreck. She's done it and I admire her for it.

She came from a comfortable background but she's proved herself as totally resilient on the road. And she's been so understanding. I haven't been easy to be with at times, but she's accepted me, faults and all. She's demonstrated the unselfishness I always saw in her. Zena would do anything for anyone, she really would.

If I end by saying she's totally loyal it makes it sound as if I've married Lassie. But that's perhaps the best of her many fine qualities – as her husband I feel totally secure in her love.

She says that she thinks it was written that we were to be together, and though I'm not a religious man that's how it feels to me too. Zena and I were supposed to be together – our love was meant to be.